Seeing GOD at Work Every Day

The Forty-Day Challenge

DAVID DENDY

WESTBOW
PRESS
A DIVISION OF THOMAS NELSON
& ZONDERVAN

WestBow Press books may be ordered through booksellers or by contacting:

WestBow Press
A Division of Thomas Nelson & Zondervan
1663 Liberty Drive
Bloomington, IN 47403
www.westbowpress.com
1 (866) 928-1240

ISBN: 978-1-4908-6883-7 (sc)
ISBN: 978-1-4908-6884-4 (hc)
ISBN: 978-1-4908-6882-0 (e)

Library of Congress Control Number: 2015901634

Print information available on the last page.

WestBow Press rev. date: 2/20/2015

Contents

Foreword

We are all running the race of life, although my two sons think I am doing a little more joggling (half jogging/half waddling) than running. Despite any aging issues that I may have, I try to focus my efforts on living life with joy and excellence.

Joy is an awesome word! It can mean a friendly smile to your spouse, laughing often, making others feel special, providing encouragement, and feeling blessed. Overall, it can be defined as bringing the spirit of God into everything you do. I think we all have felt the joy and happiness of doing something special for others, without any expectation of getting something in return. The question is, "Why don't we do it more often?"

Achieving excellence is striving to get better every day and trying to maximize our God given abilities. The famous former UCLA basketball coach, John Wooden, often stated:

> "I am not what I ought to be,
> Not what I want to be,
> Not what I am going to be,
> But I am thankful that
> I am better than I used to be."

For a number of years, I have been amazed at watching David Dendy strive for excellence, get better every day, add new skills and change his habits. I have seen him tackle piano lessons resulting in a public concert, running a marathon, and most recently writing and posting a blog every day for an entire year despite having a full time job and a very busy family. Somehow, David makes these changes and improvements seem easy and he does so with a big joyful smile on his face.

There are a number of key things that David does to help ensure that he makes it happen every time he embarks on one of these journeys for improvement. First, he publicly commits himself, by telling a significant number of people that he is going to do whatever he is challenging himself to do. Secondly, he usually gets someone to work with as a partner, confidant, teacher, or mentor to assist him along the way. Finally, David really does walk the walk of his motto of *"Fear not and Laugh often."*

What really makes David successful is his strong faith in God and daily utilization of the Bible as the best training guide ever written. He not only embarks on these journeys for God, but he does so with God. What better training partner could there be than God?

As you start the next segment of your race of life and take on the 40 Day Challenge of Seeing God At Work Every day, remember to run this race for God and others, with God and others, and have fun discovering the joy and excellence it will bring.

Doug Kintzinger
President
IMS Capital Management
Portland, Oregon
February 2015

Acknowledgments

Let me begin by thanking Gwen Ash and the great people of WestBow Press who have been patient enough with me to allow this dream to become a reality. Thank you Gwen!

Doug Kintzinger has been invaluable as a "life coach", encouraging, advising, prodding, needling, and giving me the wings to become the man I am called to be. Of course, the one thing he has taught me more than anything is that I am the one that has to do the hard work of "flapping" those wings! Thank you Doug!

To my childhood friend Doug Fields and my Youth Pastor Jim Burns who both have written a ton of Christian books. Together they have served as an inspiration to my writing and more than that they have inspired me to live my Christian life out loud! Thank you Doug and Jim!

To Leisa Chaney and Terri Ruppert who read over my manuscript and offered their expert grammatical and syntax advice! Thank you Leisa and Terri!

To Marc LeBlanc who unleashed the "author within" and gave me permission and empowered me to pursue the writing of my first book by suggesting the title of this book. Thank you Marc!

To Joni McPherson who listened and listened and then came up with the graphic design cover for the book. Your imagination and creativity are inspiring! Thank you Joni!

To those of you who constantly and consistently encouraged me to "write a book." You know who you are! This book is a direct result of your loving support! Thank you!

To my best man Cary Lothringer who is the best teacher of tennis and greatest tennis player I know. For offering me the joy of fulfilling a lifelong dream to become a Tennis Pro...Thank you Cary!

Steve Hamlin and I, over lunch one day about nine years ago vowed to one another that we would walk step by step with one another down the road of life. Nine years later we are separated by 1900 miles. But to this day we walk side by side, matching each other step for step, stride for stride. It's been quite a ride! I could not ask for a better confidant, friend, advisor, fellow sojourner and spiritual counselor! Thank you Steve!

To my children Faith and Joshua – My love for you knows no depth, no width, no height, no boundaries. You have given me but just a glimpse of the pride and love God must feel when He gazes upon His own children. Thank you Faith and Joshua!

Where would I be without Julie Keller Dendy! She found me on the way to Enchanted Rock. She believed in me when I was unbelievable. She loved me when I was unlovable. She stood by me when I wanted to sit. Julie lives up to her wedding vow – "Where you go, I will go." Believe me when I say, "We have been all over!!" Without her encouragement, her patience, her love, her incredible devotion to God and her amazing grace the book in your hands would not be. Thank you Jules!

Since I was a young man the idea of writing a book has fascinated me to no end. And now, I am an author. None of that would be possible if it were not for the Author of Life. To you O God, the One who knitted me together, the One who loves me with a furious love, the One who gently places His tender strong hands on my face and looks deep within my soul and says, "Do you know how much I love you!", to you O God I say, "Solei Deo Gloria! To You alone be the glory!" Thank you God!

Laugh often and Fear not!
David Dendy
Houston, Texas
February 2015

Introduction

I love nothing more than a good challenge! For the past few years I have had a blast with a variety of yearly challenges that have literally stretched me in ways unimaginable. From learning to play the piano, running a marathon and writing a book each challenge has taken me down unexpected roads full of potholes, speed bumps, and blind intersections all the while affording me some of the most inspiring landscapes that have enriched every fiber of my being.

The last Sunday of 2012 offered the greatest challenge to date. I was living in Dubuque, Iowa serving the University of Dubuque as the Vice President of Philanthropy at the time. On this particular Sunday morning I have to admit that my mind was wandering a bit during the sermon when God spoke to me directly and unequivocally gave voice to the challenge for the year ahead.

Write a blog every day, all year long recounting and recording where you see God at work every day in the lives of everyday people.

The only thing I had ever done consistently on a daily basis for a whole year was to go to sleep and then wake up a number of hours later. I am real good at that!

What you have before you is forty observations.
Forty recountings of seeing God at work every day.
Some will make you think.
Some will make you think I am crazy!

My hope is that with each chapter, with each observation, with each recounting, the eyes of your heart will be opened in a way that it has never been opened before.

The second half of each chapter offers an opportunity for this book to be used as an interactive journal. You will find relevant scripture quotations, reflective questions and inspiring challenges. The blank spaces left on the page are for you to record your own observations and thoughts.

Seeing God At Work Every Day– The 40 Day Challenge is just that…

A challenge to see the world around you through a lens that allows your mind, your heart and your soul to see God actively at work in your life and in the lives of the people around you.

Let the journey begin!

1

Broken

I keep hearing the same song over and over again on XM radio channel 63 - *The Message*...

The title of the song is *"Keep Making Me"* by the Sidewalk Prophets.

I hear the first line and my mind goes off into a thousand different directions and I never hear the rest of the song.

The opening line is... *"Make me broken..."*

Seeing God At Work Every Day

Why would anyone ask for that?

Pardon me, upon further reflection the phrase *"Make me broken"* in the song is not a question.

- It's a request...
- It's a plea...
- It's a desire...
- It's a hope and a wish and a command all wrapped up into one bizarre bundle.

Why not start the song with...
- *Make me whole...*
- *Make me funny...*
- *Make me popular...*
- *Make me powerful...*
- *Make me wealthy...*
- *Make me good looking...*
- *Make me ripped with six-pack abs like Zac Efron!*

I guess there's a reason that the song starts off with *"Make me broken..."*

Because we have a God who does His best work with
- broken pieces
- broken hearts
- broken dreams
- broken lives

God is the master artist at putting the pieces back together again into a majestic mosaic that is made up of just that...*broken pieces*.

I heard the song *"Keep Making Me"* by the Sidewalk Prophets just recently (again!) and I heard the completion of the opening line for the first time...

"Make me broken...
So I can be healed."

I am broken!
How about you?

Let the healing begin.
I can't wait to see what God pieces together this time.

Maybe God will use some of my broken pieces to help heal you and just maybe God will use some of your broken pieces to heal me.

And together the Master will make us into beautiful collage of interwoven broken pieces...
Maybe that's why they call us a Masterpiece!

Seeing God At Work Every Day

"God, pick up the pieces. Put me back together again."
(Jeremiah 17:14 The Message)

If you had your druthers, how would you like this sentence to be completed…

"Make me…(Feel free to use the blank space to write down your thoughts and answers)

In what ways are you "broken?"

What does your "mosaic" of broken pieces look like today? Has God been able to make a beautiful mosaic out of your broken pieces?

Reflect on this great passage from Philippians – "And I am sure of this, that he who began a good work in you will bring it to completion at the day of Jesus Christ." (Philippians 1:6 ESV)

Congratulations on starting *"Seeing God At Work Every Day - The 40 Day Challenge"*!!!

My hope and prayer is that over the next 40 days you will see God at work every day in a new light, a new angle, and in a new manner.

By reading this first chapter you are already a part of my "mosaic" and I get to be a part of yours as well. Thank you for allowing me this great privilege and pleasure of having you be a "piece" of my mosaic that God is designing. God uses the broken pieces to form the most majestic masterpieces and I have no doubt that your mosaic is just that – a Masterpiece!

I am looking forward to spending the next 40 days with you as you experience...

Seeing God At Work Every Day!!

2

The Myth of Sisyphus

Has anyone ever accused you of being "insane"?!
Me too!
The definition of insanity has been described to me with these immortal words...
"Doing the same thing over and over again expecting a different result."

Such a strong definition reminds me of the Greek mythological figure named Sisyphus who was condemned to repeat forever the same meaningless task of pushing a boulder up a mountain, only to see it roll down again.

Evidently the word Sisyphus finds its root in the word "sisyphe" - *repetition of the same meaningless task.*

Toward the end of WWII the story is told that the concentration camps in Germany were trying to conserve their bullets. In addition to trying to conserve, the camps were becoming overrun with prisoners. The leaders of the camp came up with a most brilliant and yet insidious plan to rid the camp of prisoners and yet at the same time conserve on their munitions.

A group of prisoners were told to move a very large mound of dirt from one side of the camp to the other side of the camp. Once the prisoners had accomplished the task they were told to once again move the mound of dirt back to its original location. This insane inducing "Sisyphean" task repeated itself over and over again until the prisoners, finding absolutely no meaning in their work, started throwing themselves into the electric fence that surrounded the camp only to be killed by electrocution on the spot.

Mission accomplished. Prisoner population reduced. Munitions conserved.

The Myth of Sisyphus lives on...

Seeing God At Work Every Day

You are embarking on the "40 Day Challenge to See God At Work Every Day."

If you are anything like me, you have attempted something like this before. And by about day five you stop doing "the challenge" and the book sits nicely on the shelf for years to come. A constant reminder that "Sisyphus" is alive and well.

What will be different this time around?

In the next forty days or even in the next year ahead will there be anything that will be different, add meaning and purpose to your life or will it be the same "Sisyphean" life for another year driving your mind and heart to the brink of insanity?

As mentioned above we all know the definition of insanity... *"Doing the same thing over and over again expecting a different result."*

In the book of Revelation, Jesus says: "Behold, I am making all things new... Write this down, for these words are trustworthy and true." (Revelation. 21:5 English Standard Version)

I don't know about you but I don't want this challenge ahead of us to take on the face of Sisyphus!
Let's kill the myth... Jesus is making all things new!
He even said, "Write it down, for these words are trustworthy and true."

Well...okay then.. I am writing it down - **"Jesus is making all things new!"**

I wrote it down...Now it's your turn...

Write it down!

Now... let's get out there and believe it, live it...do it!

Seeing God At Work Every Day

> And he who was seated on the throne said, "Behold, I am making all things new." Also he said, "Write it down, for these words are trustworthy and true." (Revelation. 21:5 ESV)

Let's begin this section by writing down these trustworthy words of Jesus…

What new things do you see or want to see God doing in your life?

Is there anything you can do today that will break the "Sisyphean" cycle of doing the same thing over and over and over again that absolutely drives you crazy?

See you tomorrow!

3

More than Meets the Eye

My children Faith and Joshua are now at an age where they are still learning to read and at the same time reading to learn.

My ever so creative wife, Julie engaged Faith and Joshua in a word game while she was preparing the New Year's Day breakfast. (Which was absolutely delicious!)

Julie wrote down two simple words: **NEW YEAR**

Two words, seven letters, six different letters...
She then cut up the two words into their seven individual respective letters

On another sheet of paper, underneath **NEW YEAR** she wrote the numbers 1-10 in numerical order.

The challenge was to write down as many words as possible using only the letters found in NEW YEAR. As I was watching my first thought was, "I am not sure even I can come up with ten words."

At first glance how many words do you think you can come up with?

Well, the whole family got involved in the game.
After about 10 minutes we came up with twenty-nine words!

David Dendy

Seeing God At Work Every Day

When we think that there may only be one or two or even ten different options to choose from when facing an issue, problem, situation or challenge, God just might have twenty-nine different positions, angles, or solutions in mind.

Faith and Joshua got stuck after six or seven words. With some help from some older and more experienced players (Mom and Dad) the results yielded twenty-nine words.

How many times do we try and figure out things on our own when there are more experienced and sometimes wiser people that God has placed right in our midst to help us? Seeking God and yes, seeking input from other Christian friends just might give us a wider and better perspective than we may have originally thought.

Seeing God At Work Every Day

"Where there is no guidance, a people falls,
but in an abundance of counselors there is safety." (Proverbs 11:14 ESV)
"Trust in the Lord with all your heart,
and do not lean on your own understanding.
In all your ways acknowledge him,
and he will make straight your paths." (Proverbs 3:5-6 ESV)

Is there anything going on in your life where there seems to be only one solution? Could there be more solutions or options than meets the eye?

Write down the names of some people who could serve as wise counselors for you. Call on them and seek their wisdom.

Write down the two passages above on an index card and on the back of that card write down the names of a "cabinet" - those people who can serve as wise, Christian counselors...

4

Forgiveness

I went to the bank to deposit a check. I looked in the back of the checkbook and there were no deposit slips. Lots of checks… lots of ways to spend money… lots of opportunities to get rid of money but no deposit slips… no easy way to put money into my account.

I looked at the teller with that face of improvisation and said, *"Oh, I guess I need to use one of these"* as I grabbed the generic brand deposit slip where you have to use your own pen to write down every bit of information known to you and all of your Facebook friends. I filled in every space without incidence until it came to the part known as "Account Number."

It had about 11 little rectangles where I was supposed to put my account number. *"No worries,"* I thought as I looked at a blank check with about 20 numbers on the bottom of the check. So I got started with great gusto, copying down the numbers into the 11 little rectangles. About halfway through I realized that I had more numbers than little rectangles. Sheepishly I looked up at the teller. She had a big smile on her face. *"I think I am writing down the wrong numbers,"* I confessed. Her answer was straight and to the point. *"Yes, you are."*

I reached for a new generic deposit slip. My suggestion, *"Should I just start all over?"* was quickly rebuffed with one smooth action on her part. She grabbed a little gizmo called the "Bic Wite-Out" and with three quick strokes she "whited-out" my mistakes. I stood there rather amazed. Where there was once scribble and wrong numbers, now there was just pure white space. A blank slate. I wrote down the correct numbers, slid the deposit slip over to the teller's waiting hand and within fifteen seconds my deposit was secure. I looked at her and she looked at me. She smiled. I smiled and walked out the door, laughing in spite of myself.

Seeing God At Work Every Day

With three quick strokes of the "Wite-Out" my mistakes at the Bank were wiped clean.

With three nails pounded through the body of Jesus, my mistakes in the Bank of Life were wiped clean.

In all my efforts to say, "should I start over?" or "should I do this or should I do that?", Jesus is quick in His response – "No, I've got this!" And with three nails my sins are forgiven. Jesus does that which I cannot do for myself. The forgiveness of my sins.

I look at Jesus. Jesus looks at me. He smiles, even begins to laugh. I smile and walk on, forgiveness of sins securely deposited in the Bank of Grace, humbly laughing in the amazement of it all, grateful for the one who forgives, the one who "wites-out" my sins...

Seeing God At Work Every Day

"Come now, let us reason together, says the Lord:
though your sins are like scarlet, they shall be as white as snow..."
(Isaiah 1:18 ESV)

Are there any sins, mistakes and shortcomings of your life that need to be "whited" out by the grace of Jesus? Do you have a difficult time believing that you can be made "white as snow?"

The slate has been wiped clean. You are off to a fresh start today. Offer the same grace and forgiveness to others today and watch God work in an incredible way...

Make it your aim today to seek forgiveness or offer forgiveness to at least one person...
You will have an awesome opportunity to see God at work through that type of interaction!

5

Loss

How's your year going so far?
I will never forget how one particular New Year started...

It began with a friend's husband taking his own life at work, leaving behind his beautiful wife and his two precious children ages seven and nine. To be with the new widow at her breakfast table at 9:15 a.m. only an hour after the news of her loss, with her Kleenex clenched hands on her tear stained cheeks, elbows on the table, still in her bath robe and looking across the table, her voice cracking, asking the painful question, "What do I do now?", was a moment in time where the oxygen of life was sucked out of the air and the lone heartbeat of brokenness and pain was the only sound I could hear.

Ninety minutes later we stood at the door of her mother-in-law's apartment knowing full well that as soon as that proud mom opened the door her world would be forever changed. Watching her body crumple at the inexplicable news was like watching that scene out of "Saving Private Ryan" all over again... only much worse.

Four hours later the children ran across the backyard from the yellow school bus full of "first day back to school" joy and within seconds that joy leapt from their little hearts into the abyss of anguish.

That was Tuesday, January 2nd.

David Dendy

It was only a prelude to what would take place the next day, Wednesday, January 3ʳᵈ.

At 5:15 p.m. I received a phone call with a crying voice on the other end of the line pleading for me to come to the emergency room. Upon my arrival there they were... two proud grandparents and there was the grandson, born six weeks early, oxygen deprived for over 10 minutes with the mother in ICU fighting for her life. The son of these two faithful parents was in Seattle training to be a manager. He would start driving home only to be told to stop in Portland, Oregon, where his wife and new son would be life-flighted. We held that little boy's littlest of hands and prayed and prayed...

Nine hours earlier everyone was healthy and normal. Six hours later both mother and son would be resting in the arms of Jesus. The father left behind to explain to his toddler daughter why mommy and her new baby brother weren't coming home... ever...

Ten weeks later I would leave Klamath Falls, Oregon, leaving the pastorate and becoming a Vice President at the University of Dubuque, Dubuque, Iowa.

Nine months later I am calling that year, "The Lost Year."

Lots of loss... loss of a job, loss of friends, loss of security, loss of being in a profession and calling that seemed to come so naturally, loss of spiritual identity, the loss of a home, the loss of a routine, the loss of comfortableness, the loss of being the spiritual leader of a great church, and the feeling of being lost spiritually.

So... the questions arise from many people... *"In the lostness, I cannot 'feel' God. Where did He go? Where is He? Why won't He comfort me? Why did He abandon me?"*

Have you ever asked those questions? Have you ever just asked one of those questions?

Me too...

Seeing God At Work Every Day

God is always where He always is... right there! Right next to the very soul of my heart. So close to my hand that the hairs on the back of my hand bow in reverence to His presence. So close to my broken heart that the only reason it actually beats to a rhythmic cadence is because His hands squeeze it in perfect time. So close to my buckling knees that it is only by His strong arms that He keeps me upright and enables me to place one foot in front of the other.

Oh... I may not "feel" the presence all at once but I am comforted by God's words found in

Isaiah 41...

"...You are my servant, I have chosen you and not cast you off";
fear not, for I am with you; be not dismayed, for I am your God;
I will strengthen you, I will help you.
I will uphold you with my righteous right hand." (Isaiah 41:9-10 ESV)

At the funeral of a 50 year old man whose wife is hurting beyond repair, a friend of mine sent these words to me that were used at the funeral...

"Though the voice is quiet, the Spirit echoes still..."

I have had no doubt for the last nine months that I was walking hand in hand with God and that He was leading me on a journey that is just that... a journey. On the journey there will be loss, there will be gains, there will be sadness, there will be joy, there will be mistakes, there will be hearty laughter, there will be buckets of tears, there will be forgiveness and best of all, there God will be... every step of the way, step by step... Praise be to God.

Seeing God At Work Every Day

Jesus said, "And behold, I am with you always, to the end of the age."
(Matthew 28:20 ESV)

Has there been a time in your life where you did not "feel" God's presence in your life?

Have you been able to see God at work in your life or in the life of another where there has been an experience of "loss?"

Jesus says to us, "I am with you always, to the end of the age." What comfort does that offer?

6

Affirmation

I grew up wanting to be a professional basketball player. I love the game of basketball and always thought there would come a day when I would coach a group of boys or girls in this fantastic game.

That day finally came as I coached my first basketball game for the YMCA with a team comprised of eight second graders and one first grader - my son Joshua.

We had hoped to have a practice before the first game but it was not to be.

All the boys showed up at 1:00 for our 1:30 game. We passed out jerseys, learned each other's names, ran through a few basic drills and then the referee blew his whistle, looked at me and said, "*Coach... your team ready to go?*"

My voice for some reason confidently shouted back above the fray of gym noise, "*We're ready!*" Inside I was thinking, "*Are you kidding me? I don't know what I am doing. These kids don't know what they're doing and look at all the parents, siblings and grandparents in the crowd waiting with great anticipation to see their "boy" work magic on the court under the direction of this new coach.*"

The other team ran out onto the court and they looked like giants compared to our boys. The game began with my boys running everywhere and with me shouting the encouraging words of coaching wisdom, "*Get your hands* up. Stay on your man. Pass the ball. Get back on "D" (Defense). Shoot the ball! Way to go!! Good job!"

Sometimes the boys did what I said and sometimes I thought to myself, "Do they even hear me?"

The first half ended and we had not scored one point. No ball had gone through the basket for our team. I really wondered if we would ever score.

And then it happened. One little boy threw the ball up in the air and it hung on the rim for what seem like an eternity before it dropped through the basket.

On the sidelines I came out of my shoes!!! I must have jumped six inches off the ground, threw my hands up in the air, my voice exploding in a boisterous "woohoooo", the crowd came out of their seats and then it happened...

This little boy looked straight at me with eyes that begged of, "Did I do okay Coach? Did I do good? Is that what I was supposed to do?"

My team scored four more baskets and the same thing happened with each boy. They would score a basket and their eyes shifted immediately to mine. Their bodies instinctively moved toward me.

And every time my eyes met their eyes with a look of, "Way to go! I am so proud of you! Yes!!! You did it! You did good! Well done!!"

Seeing God At Work Every Day

Have you ever thought of God as a coach? He's watching over us and there is a game plan. There are certain plays to run. There are certain boundaries to stay within.

And there we are... running all over the place. In bounds, out of bounds, shooting at the wrong basket (as did happen in our game!), not guarding our hearts and the list goes on and on.

And yet there are those times when we get it right. Out of our faith and by the power of the Holy Spirit we do it, we live it, we profess it, we honor it. We actually do and are what God has called us to be.

And do you know what I think happens next as we look to God for affirmation?

I think He comes right out of His shoes!!

Seeing God At Work Every Day

"This is my beloved Son, with whom I am well pleased."
(Matthew 3:17 ESV)

What role has "affirmation" played in your life?

Do you think of God as a God who affirms and roots for you and applauds you?

What role can you play in someone else's life by affirming and encouraging them in their journey?

Is it difficult or easy for you to let others know that you are "well pleased" with them?

Find someone to encourage today! Tell a family member or a friend or coworker that you are "well pleased" with them. I have a feeling it just might make their day. And yours, too...

7

Airplanes and Oxygen Masks

I was sitting on an airplane that was about to fly from one city to another at approximately 30,000 feet elevation with a speed of about 400-500 miles an hour.

Before the plane takes off I will hear for the 3500th time the *"Important FAA Safety Announcement"*, directing my full attention to the flight attendant at the front of the aircraft demonstrating to all those on board how to put on a seat belt.

My favorite part of the announcement is when the lead flight attendant says, *"In case of air cabin depressurization, oxygen masks will fall from the panel above you. Place the mask over your face securing the elastic band around your head."*

Now comes my favorite part... ***"And then BREATHE NORMALLY."***

So, let me get this straight. I have flown over 3500 times and the oxygen masks have never dropped down and now the one time they do indicating that the air pressure in the cabin is in serious jeopardy and the fact that the pilot is now going to have to descend to an altitude of 8,000 feet as rapidly as possible before I die of hypoxia or hypothermia (whichever comes first) I am simply to remain calm, continue reading my book, casually look out the window and BREATH NORMALLY? I think not!!

Seeing God At Work Every Day

Today and in the days ahead you will experience air cabin depressurization in your life. Something will go wrong. Leaky pipes will flood your dining room. Your children will disobey you. Your friends will disappoint you. You will become frustrated in the traffic jam. You will throw up your hands at your dysfunctional workplace. Your aging body will have some sort of breakdown. There is no getting around this.

The question becomes, *"Will I breathe normally?"* I counted fourteen normal breaths in one minute for me in a relaxed state of being. How about you? Take a minute to count...

It's the first Easter Sunday evening and the disciples don't know Jesus is risen from the dead yet. A couple of the disciples have seen the empty tomb but they don't know what has happened to Jesus. They are in a room with the doors locked for fear of the religious authorities. There are oxygen masks hanging down from the ceiling. Their world is imploding after the death of their friend and savior. The oxygen of life is being sucked out of their life and breathing normally is the furthest thing from their mind...

And then "Jesus came and stood among them and said to them, 'Peace be with you'... And when he had said this, he breathed on them and said to them, 'Receive the Holy Spirit.'" (John 20:19, 22 ESV)

When life's troubles assault us and we are tempted to panic, hyperventilate and breathe erratically, causing our very souls to faint due to the lack of oxygen, let us take in the deep breath of peace of Jesus, receive the Holy Spirit and... *"Breathe normally..."*

Seeing God At Work Every Day

"I have said these things to you, that in me you may have peace.
In the world you will have trouble. But take
heart; I have overcome the world."
(John 16:33 ESV)

Is there anything going on in your world that has caused the proverbial "oxygen masks" to drop down in front of you?

In the midst of an "air cabin depressurization" in your life, are you able to breathe normally?

Is peace simply the "absence of conflict" or is there something deeper going on when God can provide a sense of peace in the midst of conflict?

Look for someone who's got oxygen masks hanging all around them and help them "breathe normally" today with an encouraging word and prayer.

8

Quarters and Parking Meters...

I had to go downtown to get my haircut. All the downtown parking spaces have parking meters. One quarter will buy you thirty minutes of parking.

As I was approaching the building that I needed to go into I noticed that all the parking spaces directly in front of the Salon were taken, so I quickly pulled over to a parking spot one block south of my destination. I parked and started to get out of the car when I realized that the parking meter was only a 20 minute parking meter. Frustrated, I jumped back in the car, put the car in drive, crossed the street, and found a parking spot on the left side of the one way street.

Noticing I was becoming late for my appointment my fingers were having trouble finding two quarters in the console. Once the quarters were found I jumped out of the car and started to place the two quarters in the meter only to discover that my meter had one hour and forty four minutes left on the timer!

I stared at the meter in disbelief and looked on the other side of the meter to make sure I was not somehow being deceived. I actually looked around like I was on Candid Camera or something. I could not believe my good fortune.

I dropped the two quarters in my coat pocket, looked both ways (even though it was a one way street!) and crossed over to the other side of the street. As I jumped up on to the opposing curb, I had to make my way past a fancy sports car that was parked right in front of the entrance to the Salon. As I started to reach for the heavy brass doors I happened to turn and look over my left shoulder. Flashing before me in bright red lights was the word "Expired" on the parking meter for this sports car.

I started to turn back to the entrance when all of a sudden I laughed out loud and stopped dead in my tracks. I reached into my coat pocket, grabbed my two quarters and walked over to the meter and quickly dropped them into the slot to offer this sports car sixty more minutes of parking without being in jeopardy of a violation.

I quickly surveyed the area. No one in sight. I made my way into the salon with a big smile on my face and heart and got my hair cut.

Seeing God At Work Every Day

Two things struck me about this occasion...

1. The debt has been paid. I am all worried about how I am going to come up with the money to pay for the parking meter of life so that I can sufficiently pay off the debt for parking my life on this world for however many years I am going to live. I get to the meter only to discover someone else has paid the debt.

That person is Jesus!

I am in violation. My time has expired. I don't have enough quarters in this world to pay my debt. And the reality is the fact that Jesus has already paid the debt with His life on the cross and my sins are forgiven forever and ever.

The Christian life is not about what I do. It's all about what Christ has already done. He has paid the debt. We have been released, free to go, free to pursue life, free to love, free to be the person God made us to be. Praise God that Jesus has done what I could not do for myself... paid the debt.

"You are not your own, for you were bought with
a price. So glorify God in your body."
(I Corinthians 6:19-20 ESV)

2. How much fun was that to pay it forward for the owner of that sports car! Not begrudgingly, not under compulsion, not forced to do it, but rather with a skip in my step and laughter on my lips I shared the joy of being set free by passing on that good news to someone else. You can too!

Seeing God At Work Every day

"You are not your own, for you were bought with a price.
So glorify God in your body."
(1 Corinthians 6:19-20 ESV)

What is your understanding of what Jesus did on the cross?

See page 23e
Days of Awe+ Wonder - M. Borg

How do you respond to the following statement, *"The Christian life is not about what I do. It's all about what Christ has already done."*?

What does it mean to be set "free" by Jesus?

Do not only look for an opportunity today to "pay it forward" but go ahead and do it and experience the incredible joy of seeing God at work!

9

The Voice of Faith

I received an email from the school district at 5:34 a.m. letting me know that there would be a two hour delay to the start of school due to fog. I looked out the window and it was completely dark and for all I knew it was snowing. As the sun rose, sure enough - dense fog.

With the extra time in the morning we ate breakfast a little later than usual. I was standing in the kitchen when my daughter Faith casually walked by and in a very matter of fact way said, *"Daddy, can I talk to you about something?"*

Eight words from my daughter was all it took to set the ears of my heart on fire. How this daddy loves to hear the voice of his children...

I sat down opposite from Faith at the dining room table. With her big, expressive blue eyes staring right into mine she said, *"Dad, we (Faith, Joshua and Julie) were at the store yesterday and I saw this really nice necklace and I was wondering if I could get it today."*

My first thought was, *"YES! YES!! Let's go get that necklace right this moment because I love you so much and I want to give you the world and the fact that you wanted to talk to me about it just made my day, and yes honey you do have me wrapped around your little pinky in case anybody asks."*

Instead we talked about how much it cost and what the necklace looked like and what store it was at. I offered the thought that maybe she could get it for her birthday (4 months from now). She wasn't too fond of waiting that long. Eventually we left at *"We will see."* Faith said, *"OK"* and with that she swung her feet around and off the dining room bench, smiled at me and bounded off to do something else.

Julie and I talked later that evening. Faith will get the necklace for Valentine's Day. Of course, Faith does not know this, but we do. She will only have to wait one month instead of four.

Needless to say, this little conversation was everything but "little." The fact that my daughter wanted to talk to me, her Daddy, made my day. I hope and pray that we have thousands more of these *"talk to you about something"* moments.

Seeing God At Work Every Day

How the Father loves to hear the voice of His children!

Do you believe that?
Do you believe that the Father longs to hear your voice?
Do you believe that the ears of His heart are set ablaze when you utter His most majestic name?
Do you know that the Father revels and basks to be in your heart of hearts and just about falls over Himself to have "heart to heart" talks with you?
Do you know that Jesus literally (not figuratively) died to be able to talk with you voice to voice, face to face and heart to heart?
Do you believe that the fog of our lives just might give us the two hour delay we need to take a moment and say to the Lord of Lords and King of Kings, "Abba, Father can I talk to you about something?" ("Abba" means the equivalent to "Daddy" in our American vocabulary)
Do you know that you can approach His throne of grace with great confidence and with no fear and that you will be accepted just as you are at the dining table of grace?

Do you believe that the Lord delights in giving to us the desires of our hearts and that maybe, just maybe He is simply waiting for us to ask Him?

Well... maybe today you will...

"Delight yourself in the Lord, and he will give you the desires of your heart." (Psalm 37:4 ESV)

Seeing God At Work Every Day

Let us then with confidence draw near to the throne of grace,
that we may receive mercy and find grace to help in time of need."
(Hebrews 4:16 ESV)

There are eight questions above that start with *"Do you…"*
Reread those questions and respond in the space below.

If you were to approach God right this minute and say, "God, can I talk to you about something?" what would you want to talk about?

When was the last time you *"waited"* for something from God?

How the Father loves to hear the voice of His children…
Let your heavenly Father hear your voice today!

10

State Patrol Officer

Five hours driving on the road allowed me to experience a host of different weather patterns. The drive started out with bright sunshine and clear blue skies. Then I hit a huge fog bank where visibility was down to less than a quarter mile. Rain drops soon dotted my windshield. The sun quickly prevailed and I had clear sailing until the hail started. Fifteen miles from my destination the blue Rest Area sign greeted me and I pulled over to make use of the facilities. Ten yards into the exit my eyes were drawn to the rear view mirror to see the beautiful array of flashing blue lights. The Aviator Ray Ban sunglasses kept me from seeing the whites of the State Patrolman's eyes. His lips did not form a smile. They were stoically in a long straight line from left to right.

My heart sank as I grabbed for my wallet and pulled out my Iowa driver's license. *"Maybe being out of state will help my cause"*, my mind contemplated. The officer approached my passenger window and asked me how I was doing today. Really? You're asking me how I am doing after you have just pulled me over? *"Well, officer thank you for asking! Let me tell you about my day...I've seen sunshine and I've seen rain..."*

I opted for the honest approach. *"Well, officer, I am about to find out how I am doing."* We had a nice chat about how fast I was going and how the effects of "cruise control" can actually make you go faster when cresting over a hill (which is where his radar gun had clocked me going seven miles an hour over the 55 mph speed limit). He went on to offer, *"You're fine sir. Just be careful out there and be more aware of your speed."*

With that he started to move away from the vehicle. I uttered something about thank you for serving our community and sorry for your trouble...

This is about the fifteenth time I have been pulled over in my life without getting a ticket. Three minutes later I was underway driving at a speed of 5 mph below the speed limit for the rest of my journey.

I kept thinking to myself, *"When are you going to learn to simply drive the speed limit?!"*

Seeing God At Work Every Day

How fast are you driving through life these days?
How's the view? Rain? Sleet? Hail? Snow? Sunshine?
When was the last time you pulled over to rest?
When was the last time someone had to pull you over to get your attention?

I have a feeling had I not turned into the Rest Area the State Patrolman would have pulled me over just a little bit further down the road.

Is there someone in your world, in your life that has that unique ability to pull you over and say, *"Hey, slow down. Be a little more aware of what's going on. Take some time to rest and gather yourself. What you're doing right now is not best for you and others. Please take some corrective action."*

That "someone" is many times God's word for me.

One of my Seminary professors would always say, *"Sometimes scripture corrects our thinking..."* I always liked that.

"All Scripture is breathed out by God and profitable for teaching, for reproof, for correction, and for training in righteousness, that the man of God may be complete, equipped for every good work." (2 Timothy 3:16-17 ESV)

Thank you for journeying through life with me.

Thank you for pulling over and resting for a moment with me today.

Now, let's get back out there and be aware of God's word and God's grace so that we may be complete and equipped for the day and the journey ahead!

Seeing God At Work Every Day

"All Scripture is breathed out by God and profitable for teaching,
for reproof, for correction, and for training in righteousness,
that the man of God may be complete, equipped for every good work."
(2 Timothy 3:16-17 ESV)

When was the last time you were pulled over and told to slow down?

Take a moment to collect your thoughts on your life. Is there anything that needs to be corrected?

Is there a person or group of friends that you can count on to help you slow down and rest?

Pick up the phone, send the text, write the email today and connect with that person or group today...

11

Shift Happens

The delightful flight attendant's voice echoed the same announcement that I have heard on every flight since the day I was born. The warning came right after we landed.

"Please be careful when opening the overhead bins as contents may have shifted during the flight."

Seeing God At Work Every Day

Shift Happens...

It happens to all of us. No one is exempt. "Shift" is not discriminatory. The contents of everyone's life shifts at one time or another.

"Oh, I will never get divorced," we say. Fifteen years later we find ourselves single again.

"Those homeless people just don't have a good work ethic," we pontificate. Next thing we know we have been given the pink slip and within two months our savings has dried up and the house is going into foreclosure with nowhere to go.

"I exercise every day. I am in great shape," we say with confidence. Cancer sometimes doesn't care if you exercise or don't before it decides to strike.

Children disobey and run off to do their own thing. Friends are fickle. Families are finicky. Occupations can be hazardous. Car accidents happen. I could go on all day.

Air turbulence causes the contents of our life to be shifted.

So, what do we do when we open the overhead bin of life and discover that the contents have shifted?

We look to the one who has not shifted!

In a great storm on the sea, the disciples of Jesus were panicking as their dispositions and egos were being shifted. But it was Jesus who was "still and solid" in the storm, unshifted by the waves and the tempest. Jesus was at peace in the midst of the storm.

"And they went and woke him, saying, 'Master, Master, we are perishing!' And he awoke and rebuked the wind and the raging waves, and they ceased, and there was a calm. He said to them, 'Where is your faith?'" (Luke 8:24-25 ESV)

In a moment Jesus stilled the storm.

There are times when Jesus calms the tempest.
And then there are times when Jesus calms you.

May Jesus still the storm of your world today and in the process may He still you too.

Shift Happens!

And guess what?

Jesus happens too...

Seeing God At Work Every Day

"And they went and woke him, saying, 'Master, Master, we are perishing!'
And he awoke and rebuked the wind and the
raging waves, and they ceased,
and there was a calm. He said to them, 'Where
is your faith?'" (Luke 8:24-25 ESV)

Has there been any major "shift" in your life recently?

When we experience "shifting storms" where does our focus tend to be?
On the Storm or on the Savior?

What storms or "shifts" can Jesus calm in your life today?

What would life look like if Jesus calmed you today?

12

The Wall

During my Junior High years I began to discover my musical tastes. "Frampton Comes Alive" was my first "rock" album. Then came Boz Scaggs, Boston, Styx and then Kansas! I loved Kansas. First came "Leftoverture" with "Carry On Wayward Son" followed by "The Point of Know Return" with the epic acoustic classic, "Dust in the Wind." If you're younger than 40 years of age you might want to look up these classics on YouTube.

As everyone was carried away with the first song of the "Leftoverture" album "Carry On Wayward Son", it was the second song which captivated me and to this day is an often played song on my iTunes.

It's called **"The Wall."**

Kerry Livgren writes and sings about "The Wall," an immovable object that his life has led him to and how his life has now come to a standstill. I offer to you the second verse...

To pass beyond is what I seek, I fear that I may be too weak
And those are few who've seen it through to glimpse the other side,
The promised land is waiting like a maiden that is soon to be a bride
The moment is a masterpiece, the weight of indecision's in the air
It's standing there, the symbol and the sum of all that's me
It's just a travesty, towering, blocking out the light and blinding me
I want to see

I hit a wall recently. I had been circling it for weeks, maybe even months, sizing it up, looking for my way around it, over it, under it and today I discovered that there is only one way... through it.

I slump against it. Its cold slab chills me to the bone. The wall absorbs nothing. My tears trickle, cascading down it glassy surface, pooling at my feet. The Wall's laughter echoes off its gray granite as my pounding fists bounce off of it. I make not a dent. It towers. It intimidates. It chuckles in its premature self-declared victory dance. The scattered skeletons of those who have flailed and failed have front row seats to my futility.

The odds makers are at it again.
Who will break who? Does the Wall break me or do I break the Wall?
The song pumps through my veins:
"To pass beyond is what I seek, I fear that I may be too weak.
And those are few who've seen it through to glimpse the other side."

Seeing God At Work Every Day

It's not the first Wall I have run into in my life.
It won't be my last.
It's just the next one in line.

So it is for you. It may seem taller, wider, thicker, and denser but in the end it's just another Wall.

Our God is an awesome wall breaker. He makes
- obsidians obsolete,
- saprolite superfluous,
- pumice into pebbles and
- granite into granules.

If we believe that God has called us to where we are and to where we need to be then nothing, nothing can withstand His will and His way. Look out Wall, I'm coming through...

David Dendy

And David said to the Wall of a man named Goliath,

> "I come to you in the name of the Lord of
> hosts... This day the Lord will deliver
> you into my hand, and I will strike you down..."
> (1 Samuel 17:45-46 ESV)

ps... See you on the other side...

Seeing God At Work Every Day

"…I come to you in the name of the Lord of hosts…
This day the Lord will deliver you into my
hand, and I will strike you down…"
(1 Samuel 17:45-46 ESV)

How would you describe the walls that you have run into lately?

Will these walls defeat you or will you, with God's help, strike them down?

Make a list of the "walls" that God has gotten you through…

13

Compliments

Compliment - *an expression of praise, commendation or admiration*

I received two of these recently. They really boosted my morale and countenance for the day. Not only did they boost me, they carried me. People asked how my day was going and I said, *"Great!"* How could it not be going great! Two people had just offered me "expressions of praise, commendation and admiration."

Seeing God At Work Every Day

Here's my question... to myself.

I will let you listen in on this conversation...

"Would I have had a "great" day if I had not received those two compliments? Is my having a great day or a poor day dependent on whether or not I receive compliments? Aren't you being pretty shallow David? Surely you have a better foundation than that! Are you now going to go around doing "good deeds" so that you can receive compliments so that you can have a "great day?"

I think you have heard enough little tidbits from what goes on inside my mind...

What I have discovered over the years is that we are a people who long for acceptance, appreciation and accolades.

What has troubled me the most over the years is how stingy most people are in giving out compliments to others.

I was 43 years old before I heard from my dad that he was *"proud of me."* I told him that I needed to know if he was proud of me. He said he was. To his credit, for the last four years of his life each conversation we had ended with him saying, *"I'm proud of you, Son."*

I guess my take is that if Jesus needed to hear that His Father was proud of him, then maybe we need to offer these kind of compliments and admiration to others as well.

Try it today. See how many sincere compliments you can dish out today.

I have a feeling you are going to really help someone have a "great day!"

One more thing... I bet you are going to have a "great day" too!

Seeing God At Work Every Day

"And when Jesus was baptized, immediately he went up from the water,
and behold, the heavens were opened to him, and
he saw the Spirit of God descending
like a dove and coming to rest on him; and
behold, a voice from heaven said,
'This is my beloved Son, with whom I am well
pleased.'" (Matthew 3:16-17 ESV)

Are you typically generous or stingy with compliments to others?

How do you handle receiving compliments?

Dish out as many sincere compliments as you can today. Write down what you discover.

14

David vs. Gorilla!

Faith and Joshua had their newly designed race cars participate in the Pinewood Derby.

A couple of days prior to the race we had taken Faith and Joshua over to Mr. Johnson's "Mini Home Depot" shop on Saturday and had these blocks of wood transformed into racing cars. The cars were designed. The cars were painted. The cars had little "Lego" people on them to add an atmosphere of authenticity. All that was left to make the cars a finished product was to put the axles and the wheels on the cars. Faith and Joshua went to bed on Tuesday night with the full anticipation of seeing the completed product when they woke up the next morning.

We put the kids to bed, retreated to the kitchen, caught up from the day and about 9:00 o'clock the "simple" procedure of adding the axles and wheels began. You know where this is going, don't you?!

I was quite proud of myself that at 9:28 p.m. I had admitted defeat and called Mr. Johnson. He chuckled and said something about *"this sometimes"* happens. I thought to myself, *"No, it doesn't. It only happens to me."* As expected, he offered great advice and I was off and running, well actually "continued stumbling."

Mr. Johnson mentioned that after securing the axles in place, you might want to add a little glue for extra security. No problem. Julie brought out a brand new package of "Gorilla Glue" that had never been opened.

I ripped open the package, twisted off the cap and squeezed the bottle. It was hard as a rock. Julie forgot to mention that this new bottle was a few years old. Not to be deterred, I grabbed the power drill and made an opening... in the side of the bottle! I began to squeeze and out this glue came, dripping everywhere... all over my fingers, and the kitchen counter top. The Gorilla Glue eventually made its way to the axles and after twenty minutes the project was complete.

All ten of my fingers were as sticky as they could be. They were so sticky, they started to literally stick to one another. I quickly turned on the hot water, rubbed some soap in there and grabbed a paper towel. My fingers were just as sticky. The situation was growing worse rather than better.

I asked Julie to look up on Google on her iPad, *"How to get Gorilla Glue off your hands."* Her response was classic, *"Are you serious?"* YES, I am serious. I stood over the kitchen sink, with fingers spread wide, awaiting the answer.

Julie found a website and then began to read the instructions. She got as far as... *"Don't use hot water..."* and then started laughing so hard all I heard was something about "sandpaper, olive oil, pumice stone, exfoliation, don't use gasoline and should your "digits" get stuck please see a doctor."

Doubled over, Julie found a pumice stone and a bottle of olive oil and there I stood for the next 30 minutes trying to sand down the Gorilla Glue off of my fingers and all the while trying to preserve my God given unique fingerprints. I looked around and Jesus was nowhere to be found. I lost Him between the second and third axle! I think He was off somewhere laughing too...

Seeing God At Work Every Day

Is this not one of the reasons we don't get involved in other people's business and lives?

People and their lives are like an unopened package of Gorilla Glue.

We notice they need help. We offer assistance. Or they ask us for help. And we are happy to respond and before we know it, we are stuck in a sticky mess that we cannot get off of our hands. The more we try to assist the stickier the situation becomes.

Here's the axiom of the day... People are sticky. People are messy. People can be a real pain. People take time. People don't easily wash off of our hands or our hearts.

Here's the second axiom of the day... People are worth helping. People are worth investing in. Messy, sticky fingers is a small price to pay for helping someone run the race and receive the reward of crossing the Finish Line.

After all, Jesus knows all about getting stuck. He got himself stuck to a cross in order to make sure we could run the race set before us and not only run... but to cross the Finish line.

At the end of the Pinewood Derby Joshua had won one race. Faith stood next to her trophy for "Most Creative Car." The smile on their faces and the joy in their heart was worth the sticky fingers.

It always is...

David Dendy

Seeing God At Work Every Day

Read the Parable of the Good Samaritan found in Luke 10:29-37

What are some of the reasons we don't get involved in other people's business?

What are some of the reasons we "do" get involved in other people's business?

God just might use you to be the "Gorilla Glue" to help keep the "axles on" for someone. Be on the lookout today for someone who might be "stripped... beat...and left for half dead."!

15

Open Doors

A little after 5:00 p.m. I walked up to the front doors of the elementary school where my children go to school. They were in "aftercare" - a YMCA sponsored after school program that is offered for parents who are not able to pick up their children right when school lets out.

As I approached I noticed a couple looking through the front doors with cupped hands around their faces. They proceeded to push the intercom button. Quickly the lady pulled out her cell phone and started to dial the school's phone number. The husband kept rhythmically "bobbing" back and forth from looking through the glass and looking at his wife.

My stomach went into a bit of a panic as I thought perhaps I had shown up too late and "aftercare" was over and my kids had been shipped to DHS. I approached the front doors, looked at the couple and then proceeded to say, *"Are the doors locked?"* At that moment I placed my hand on the door handle and pulled...

Voila!! The door opened!

The man looked at me as if I had some sort of super power and the lady quickly put away her "flip" phone. His comment was an instant classic - *"I thought the doors were locked. I never actually tried to open it."*

David Dendy

I smiled and said, *"Come on in."*

Seeing God At Work Every Day

How many times have I heard someone say something to this effect, *"Well... when God closes one door, He opens another?"*

After yesterday I am starting to rethink that old adage.

What if there were lots of doors that God provided for me and I never went through those doors for the simple reason, *"I thought the doors were locked. I never actually tried to open it!!!"*

Perhaps today we might want to try and open some doors that God has placed in front of us and actually "go through" those doors and start a new God endorsed adventure!

Or perhaps we can stand outside and huddle together, with our cell phones out, looking through the glass, impatiently waiting and wondering, *"How much longer until God opens the door for us?"*

Seeing God At Work Every Day

Jesus said, "I am the door. If anyone enters by me, he will be saved and will go in and out and find pasture." (John 10:9 ESV)

Are there any doors in your past that you thought were locked but in retrospect perhaps you never tried to open them?

What doors might God be encouraging you to pull the handle on and see if they are unlocked?

What keeps us from trying to open "closed doors?" Have you ever tried to "pick" the lock of a closed door? (Me too!)

Pull on a few door handles today and see where God might be leading you...

16

The Dimmer Switch

His demeanor was lower than an alligator's belly.
Her countenance had fallen faster than the Twin Towers.
I have seen these postures a thousand times. So have you.
A person's self-esteem, confidence in their abilities, and overall attitude toward themselves is basically in the toilet.
What does one say? What advice or counsel can be offered?

I have used the analogy of "The Dimmer Switch" hundreds of times.

The powerful underlying question is...
"Who is in control of the "Dimmer Switch" of the light bulb of your life?"

Seeing God At Work Every Day

I am convinced that God has made all of our lives to shine with the brightness of a 500 watt light bulb.

However, I am also convinced that most people live their lives with the brightness of 60-100 watts.

Why?

Most people have allowed someone and it could be anyone to have control over the "Dimmer Switch" of their lives.

How many relationships have I seen where one "spouse/significant other/ family member" has complete control of the dimmer switch and for reasons that are not all together completely clear to me or to anyone else in the universe, this person holds the dimmer switch down to a level that the person in question barely makes a glimmer.

How many people have I seen hold down the "Dimmer Switch" on their own lives because someone told them, *"Don't shine too bright. Don't be a bright and shining star. You're making everyone else around you look bad. You're nothing. You're a nobody."* And the list goes on and on.

I ran across this quote years ago that is worth sharing today and tomorrow and the next day...

"Our deepest fear is not that we are inadequate. Our deepest fear is that we are powerful beyond measure. It is our light, not our darkness that most frightens us. We ask ourselves, Who am I to be brilliant, gorgeous, talented, fabulous? Actually, who are you not to be? You are a child of God. Your playing small does not serve the world. There is nothing enlightened about shrinking so that other people won't feel insecure around you. We are all meant to shine, as children do. We were born to make manifest the glory of God that is within us. It's not just in some of us; it's in everyone. And as we let our own light shine, we unconsciously give other people permission to do the same. As we are liberated from our own fear, our presence automatically liberates others." (*Marianne Williamson - excerpt from Return to Love...1992*)

Here's my twofold word for the day...

1. Get your hand off the Dimmer Switch and let God turn it up. Don't settle for 60 or even 100 watts. Shine bright my friend... Shine Bright!!
2. If someone else has their hand on your "Dimmer Switch"... slap their hand so hard that it makes their head spin. You've got some shining to do!

David Dendy

Jesus said, "I am the light of the world. Whoever follows me will not walk in darkness, but will have the light of life." (John 8:12 ESV)

Turn it up!
Light up the world!
Let the light of God in you shine bright today!!

Seeing God At Work Every Day

Jesus said, "I am the light of the world. Whoever follows me
will not walk in darkness, but will have the light of life." (John 8:12 ESV)

Who is in control of the "Dimmer Switch" of your life?

What will it take to let God be in control of your "Dimmer Switch?"

Has anyone ever told you not to shine too bright? If so, how has that impacted
your life?

What would happen if by following Jesus the light of your life would shine
at 500 watts?

What are some practical steps you can take today to begin to allow God to take hold of the Dimmer Switch of your life?

Go to www.biblegateway.com and type in the word "light" under key word search. Read a bunch of the verses it lists. The word "light" is mentioned 277 times in the Bible I read. I would say that is pretty significant!

17

Wing Nut...

The restaurant didn't open until 11:00 a.m. and I was there at 10:55 and the doors were locked.
I waited outside basking in the sunshine allowing the rays to warm my body.
In my peripheral vision I saw a homeless man with a large duffel bag strapped to his back start moving my way.
I knew he would stop and ask for a handout and my prediction did not go unfulfilled.

He made some joke toward me and started cackling and I started laughing because it seemed the appropriate thing to do.

He almost walked by me but my curiosity wouldn't allow it. I said, "Hey! What are you doing?"

He drew closer so that we were standing within a foot or two from each other. Over the years I have run into a number of people who are homeless and they carry with them a certain aroma. It is distinct, unique and unforgettable.

He said, *"I am heading to Winnemucca. My mom is on her deathbed and I need to go and see her."* (*Winnemucca is only about 300 miles away!!*) He continued, *"Do you have any money that might help me out?"*

Without hesitating I grabbed for my wallet and asked, "How much do you need?" He kind of just shrugged. With my eyes big and wide I offered, *"How about a twenty?"* His eyes sparkled. They twinkled. They danced. And then they became as genuine and sincere as they could be as he shook my hand and said, *"Thank you...Thank you so much."*

I inquired, *"What is your name?"*
He replied, *"My name is Mickey but everyone calls me Wing Nut!"*
"Wing Nut?" I asked with a huge smile on my face.

"Yes, that's the name I got on the streets."

Wing Nut lives on the streets. He has for the last twenty years. I asked him how he survives and he said by generous people like me. He makes a phone call every so often to touch base with family. Wing Nut is 43 years old and he looks more like 73.

Whiskers cover his entire face and ears. He stands about 5 feet 7 inches tall. His hair is sun bleached and wiry. His smile is wide, with a number of missing teeth along with the chewing tobacco stuck between his bottom lip and teeth. His left foot is numb and he has a number of plates and screws to hold his body together.

I said to Wing Nut, *"I am a praying man and I am going to be praying for your safety and that you get to see your mom."* (He hadn't seen her in ten years)

He looked at me as a brother looks at his own brother and said, *"Well, I have my Bible in my bag. I love the Psalms. I have learned so much from the Psalms."*

We chatted another minute or two and it was time for him to go meet some folks who were going to offer him a job. He wasn't sure he was going to take it or not.

We hugged each other tightly and then he started to walk away and then he stopped.

He made a quarter turn, looked at me, smiled widely and said, *"David... We will see each other again."* And off he went...

We sure will Wing Nut... We sure will...

Seeing God At Work Every Day

Jesus offers these words, "Truly, I say to you, as you did it to one of the least of these my brothers, you did it to me." (Matthew 25:40 ESV)

Of the two people in the encounter above, who would you say was more blessed?
Wing Nut or David Dendy?

The answer seems obvious to me...

Thank you Wing Nut for doing unto one of the least of these your brothers!! I was blessed by you reaching out to me!! And I know Jesus is smiling for you ministering to me in His name.

May I do the same to others...

Seeing God At Work Every Day

"Truly, I say to you, as you did it to one of the least of these my brothers, you did it to me." (Matthew 25:40 ESV)

Have you run into any "Wing Nuts" lately?

Keep your eyes peeled today for "one of the least of these" and discover how you might be a real blessing to each other.

When we look to bless others, many times we are the ones who receive the greatest blessing...

18

The Most Profound Question...

For the last fifteen years Julie and I have kept a most wonderful, fun and blessed practice.

About once or twice a year we will offer a very large tip to a waiter or waitress of our choosing.

The perfect scene was set as we dined at the Main Street Chophouse.

Our server for the evening introduced himself as Josh.

I said, *"Hello Josh, my name is David and this is Julie."*

He had dirty blonde hair cut short on the sides and messy on the top.

His eyes were so expressive in describing the specials of the night.

He used his hands in great animated ways in describing the entrees.

I noticed a very endearing habit of Josh's throughout the night. He would ask how everything was tasting and we would enthusiastically respond, *"Great Josh! Everything is fantastic."*

And then we would take his right hand and tap it on the table in three quick successions and then while moving on he would do the same to the side of the booth while saying, *"Ok..."*

I don't think we were ten minutes into the dinner and Julie looked up at me and said, *"Tonight is the night and Josh is the one."*

I knew in an instant what she meant.
And so it was.

We enjoyed our dinner, laughed and cried in talking about my trip back to Klamath Falls, Oregon and all the wonderful friends and memories we made there.

And then came the bill. I offered my credit card and Josh was quick in returning the bill for me to sign.

I looked him square in the eye and I said the following:

"Josh... Julie and I have been very blessed this year in our lives and we want to pass on some of that blessing to others. And tonight... you're the one! I would like to offer you a $100 tip."

Josh's eyes got real big and in a dumbfounded way said, *"You don't have to do that."*

I said, *"I know I don't have to. But I want to. You're the one, Josh!"*

And then...

Josh leaned forward with those big expressive eyes with his hands outstretched in disbelief and asked the most profound question...

"Why am I the one?"

Seeing God At Work Every Day

This is the joy and delight that God has for us!

Out of His free will, out of His great love, God has chosen us to redeem, to save, to love and to bless.

And we ask with dumbfounded disbelief... **"Why am I the one?"**

It's not because we are handsome and pretty.
It's not because we are pathetic and needy.
It's not because we do great things.
It's not because we do terrible things.

It's not because we are just the nicest, most loving, caring people in the whole wide world.
It's not because we serve the needy, clothe the naked, house the homeless and feed the hungry.
This list could go on and on...

Like Josh, we ask in dumbfounded disbelief, *"Why am I the one?"*

Here's the answer and it is the only answer to the most profound question...

Because God loves you...

Seeing God At Work Every Day

"For you are a people holy to the Lord your God. The Lord your
God has chosen you to be a people for his treasured possession,
out of all the peoples who are on the face of the earth. It was not
because you were more in number than any other people that
the Lord set his love on you and chose you, for you were the
fewest of all peoples, but it is because the Lord loves you..."
(Deuteronomy 7:6-8 ESV)
"We love because he first loved us." (1 John 4:19 ESV)

Ponder for a moment the fact that God loves you...regardless of anything
you have done or not done...

Where do we get the idea that we have to somehow "earn" God's love?

Choose someone today to do something out of the ordinary...just because...

God has chosen you and loves you out of His great love and grace! Bask in
that today!

19

First Day of Camp!

The whole family went over to Camp Albrecht Acres to help check in the campers arriving for their weeklong adventure.

Faith and Joshua and I were helping the campers with their luggage, making sure it got to the right cabin. Julie was in charge of the "Bank" - keeping track of the camper's money for the week ahead. Most campers deposited five to ten dollars in the "Bank."

I loved observing the campers coming into the registration building.

Some were nervous.

Others excited.

Some recognizing other campers from years past with shouts of *"hello"* and big hugs.

Others arrived with pensive outlooks as this was their first time.

Most of the campers were accompanied by their parents.

Sometimes I couldn't tell who was more nervous... the parents or the children.

I met Emily's dad... shook his hand and said, *"We'll take good care of your girl this week."* He nodded his head in the most subtle of ways with his cowboy hat barely making a move.

Ricky came up to me and said, *"Hi... I'm Wicky."* He shook my hand then extended his arms way up in the air for a "Welcome to Camp" hug.

Gwen arrived and she was rather stunning. Long legs, big smile and her arms were ripped (as in great muscle tone).

Chris arrived with his Chicago White Sox hat on and he kept going on and on about the White Sox.

Richard was so sweet. He drew me two pictures while I was helping.

Sarah had the deepest onyx colored eyes that were simply captivating.

Oops... Forgive me... I left out one important detail of Camp Albrecht Acres.

This camp is for adults who have special needs.

The campers ranged from 18 to 60 years in age.

Emily has Down Syndrome and her parents are the sweetest couple you would ever meet.

Ricky has Down Syndrome and has a great sense of humor and gives great hugs!

Gwen is wheelchair bound and her long legs are so twisted and contorted, I am not sure that they will ever stop from being crisscrossed. Her arms are "ripped" because she flexes her arms with great intensity about every twenty seconds. Her big smile was only interrupted by her second and third finger of her left hand that was constantly being sucked on.

Chris kept asking me my name and latched onto the fact that I even knew who the Chicago White Sox were.

Richard, in his 50's was the "silent" artist. He would come up to me and hand me a picture he had just drawn with crayons and then shuffle back to his table. Before long... there he was again...with another work of art.

And then there was Sarah... (Tears cascade down my face as I think about Sarah)

Sarah is in a wheelchair. Her feet are in a locked position. Her hands are palms down on the armrests. Neither her feet nor her hands moved the whole time I saw her.

Her head ticks to the left and then tocks back to the center in perfect rhythm like a metronome.

She was sitting in her room with her counselor by her side when I brought in her luggage.

I politely asked, *"Are you Sarah?"*

The counselor said, *"Yes..."*

I looked straight into Sarah's beautiful onyx colored eyes and gently said, *"Sarah. I hope you are going to have a great week at camp."*

Her head tilted to the left and then back to center and then back to the left and then back to center....

I gazed at Sarah...

I don't think Sarah saw me... but then again maybe she did... I don't know... I never will...She was captivating nonetheless...One thing I do know... I saw Sarah and maybe that's all that matters...

Seeing God At Work Every Day

I am not sure what to say about my experience on that warm Sunday afternoon at Camp Albrecht Acres.

I am sure of one thing though...

I was on Holy Ground.

There was something about knowing the Campers by name that transcended their special needs.

David Dendy

Thank you Lord for giving me the privilege of serving
Rachel, Tiffany, Kevin, Gwen, Ricky, Tom, Richard, Chris, Mitt, Emily,
Nikitta, Chase and of course... Sarah.

There were many more...whose names I cannot remember.
And here's the good news... God knows their names!

And He knows ours too...and maybe that's all that matters...

"Fear not, for I have redeemed you;
I have called you by name, you are mine." (Isaiah 43:1 ESV)

P.S. - And to the counselors who have the privilege of serving these campers
all week long until another group shows up next Sunday... May God richly
bless you and your life for your love and care for those that society so often
forgets and pushes off to the side.
Thank you thank you thank you thank you thank you thank you thank you...

Seeing God At Work Every Day

"Fear not, for I have redeemed you;
I have called you by name, you are mine."
(Isaiah 43:1 ESV)

What is it about being called by name that is so powerful?

I love the fact that God calls us and knows us by name!

Work on calling people by name today and see what a difference it makes in how you perceive others....

20

Met Any Interesting Women Lately?

I watched a poignant video that struck me to the core.
Actor and Academy Award winner Dustin Hoffman was sharing the most important lesson he learned from playing the role of a woman in one of the top ranked comedy movies of all time: **"Tootsie."**

Before the movie went into production Dustin Hoffman asked the make-up artists at Columbia Pictures to "make him up" into a woman. If he could walk down the streets of New York and not be looked upon as a man who was in drag then he would do the movie. He really wanted to look like a woman.

The make-up artists went to work...
Sure enough, the make-up artists succeeded.
Upon returning from venturing out onto the streets of New York Dustin Hoffman looked in the mirror and said to the make-up artists, "You have done a great job of making me look like a woman. Now, I need you to make me look like a beautiful woman."

The reply was sobering... *"This is as good as it gets."*

Dustin went home and told his wife with tears running down his face, *"I have to make this picture."* She asked, *"Why?"*

Listen carefully to Dustin's response...

"Because I think I am an interesting woman when I look at myself on the screen. And I know that if I met myself at a party I would never talk to that character because she doesn't fulfill physically the demands that we are brought up to think that women have to have in order for us to ask them out."
My wife asked, "What are you saying?"
"There are too many interesting women that I have... I have... I have not had the experience to know in this life because I have been brainwashed. That (Tootsie) was never a comedy for me."

Seeing God At Work Every Day

The prophet Samuel is brought to the house of Jesse to pick the new king. Jesse brings out more than a handful of sons and Samuel is immediately drawn to the oldest, first born son. Just look at him... He's tall, he's handsome, he's strong! Yes, he is the one!

Listen carefully to the Lord's response...
"Do not look on his appearance or on the height of his stature, because I have rejected him. For the Lord sees not as man sees: man looks on the outward appearance, but the Lord looks on the heart." (1 Samuel 16:7 ESV)

And Samuel takes a look at each succeeding son and the Lord keeps saying, "No."
Exasperated, Samuel asks Jesse, *"Do you have any other sons?"*

Jesse basically responds, *"Oh yes...I nearly forgot... I do have one more son out in the fields tending my sheep. I'll go get him."*

Upon Jesse's return with young ruddy looking shepherd boy David, Samuel is filled with God's spirit and declares, *"He's the one."*

David is anointed right on the spot and eventually becomes king and was ultimately declared to be a *"man after God's own heart."*

My hope and prayer is this...

David Dendy

Today and tomorrow and the next day and the next one after that...may the Lord open the eyes of our hearts not only to see, but to meet and get to know some very _**"interesting"**_ people who are ultimately men and women after God's own heart.

76

Seeing God At Work Every Day

"Do not look on his appearance or on the height of
his stature, because I have rejected him.
For the Lord sees not as man sees: man looks on the outward appearance,
but the Lord looks on the heart."
(1 Samuel 16:7 ESV)

What steps can you take to begin looking past the external and seeing the real heart of the people you meet?

Are there some "interesting" people in your life that you have overlooked because they do not meet certain "stereotypical" standards?

Pray for the Lord to "open the eyes of your heart" to see others as He sees them…

21

See You On The Other Side...

As part of a team building exercise our whole staff went "Zip Lining."
If you have never been on a "Zip Line" it provides lots of entertainment as well as building your own sense of trust in equipment and in people as you "zip" through the air suspended 45 feet above the ground on a very thin cable. As we were getting ready to go on one of the zip lines our guide led the way and as she embarked she shouted, *"See you on the other side."*

Seeing God At Work Every Day

Not two hours after completing the Zip Line experience I received a text message from a good friend of mine who was fifteen minutes outside of town "just passing through."
My friend is home from deployment. He's been on three deployments in the last five years. He is a fighter pilot and serving our country with great pride and expertise.
We met at church in Klamath Falls, Oregon a few years ago. He was learning how to fly the F-15 Eagle fighter jet. He loves the Lord.
He is a tall, chiseled hunk of a man and when he pulled up on his brand new "blacked out" Harley Davidson motorcycle with his four day growth beard and his bandana on his head, I have to say, my heart was just a little bit envious.

His quick smile and warm embrace was met with the same and even though we hadn't seen each other in four years, it was as if we had never been apart. We drove over to the University of Dubuque campus and grabbed a waffle cone of Rocky Road ice cream at Mike and Betty's Ice Cream shop. We quickly found ourselves sitting under the Bell Tower on the quad enjoying the summer breeze.

My friend is hurting... grieving the loss of his marriage of five and a half years...
Feeling "burned"... "distrustful"... "at a loss of how to begin anew"...

I know those feelings.
I have been through those firsthand.
He's crawling down a road that I have paved with my hands and knees as well.

We talked...
We shared...
I shared with him the verse that changed my life when I went through my divorce...
"I know the plans I have for you," declares the Lord, "plans to prosper you and not to harm you, plans to give you hope and a future." (Jer. 29:11 New International Version)

We were vulnerable...
We laughed...
We prayed...
We hugged...
We took pictures...
He started up the Harley, made a sharp left turn out of the parking lot and roared off...

One thing that I told him with incredible confidence, trust and experience was this...
"Josh... there's life on the other side of divorce."

David Dendy

He looked at me...
I looked at him...
I'm on the other side...
He's not.... yet...

"Hey Josh! See you on the other side!"

Seeing God At Work Every Day

"I know the plans I have for you," declares the Lord,
"plans to prosper you and not to harm you, plans to give
you hope and a future." (Jeremiah 29:11 NIV)

Think of a difficult period in your life where you came through to the "other side."

Do you know of anyone who is going through a similar time in their own life? Reach out to them and encourage them that with God's help there is "life on the other side."

Write Jeremiah 29. 11 down on ten index cards. Keep them with you. Memorize the verse. Be ready to share it with people you meet. You will be amazed how many times this verse will be of comfort to someone you talk with. Hand them one of the index cards as an encouraging gesture that the Lord has great plans to get them to the other side!

22

The Arithmetic of a Healthy Relationship

Two fine looking young "twenty somethings" descended upon our home from Milwaukee, Wisconsin with one purpose... to ask me if I would officiate their marriage ceremony on May 3, 2014. Nicole is my wife Julie's cousin's daughter... Dustin is the groom to be.

I have known Nicole for close to 15 years and I have a rather discerning eye and a big baseball bat when it comes to the men who want to court her. Dustin need not worry! What fun to sit with the two of them and watch them interact with one another, me, Julie, Faith and Joshua.

We started talking about what makes a relationship "healthy."
I looked at them and said, *"It's simple arithmetic for a healthy relationship."*

Dustin, as an accountant got all excited. Believe it or not, as an accountant he really does have a personality!!

Seeing God At Work Every Day

Let's take a look at general arithmetic...

We have....
- Addition...
- Subtraction...
- Multiplication...
- Division...
- Fractions...

Here are some simple questions to ask yourself in regards to any relationship with any person...

1. **Addition** - Does this person "add" good characteristics to your being and to your life? Are you "more" of who you are when you are with this person?
2. **Subtraction** - Does this person "subtract" or "take away" the important characteristics of your being that make you, uniquely you? Are you "less" of who you are when you are with this person?
3. **Multiplication** - Does this person "multiply" your friendships, acquaintances, family connections, hobbies, interests and desires in life?
4. **Division** - Does this person "divide" you from your family, your friends, your interests, your hobbies, your gifts, your talents, your skills?
5. **Fractions** - We are always just a fraction of being "whole." In order to become "whole" you need to have a "common denominator" with another person so that the two of you can be added up to make "one." What is the common denominator you have with this other person? Drinking? Great sex? Bar hopping? Sports? Work? Neighbors? Children? Gambling? Hobbies? Special interests? The love of Jesus?

Nicole and Dustin... I do believe that this relationship "adds" up to something great!!

I would be more than privileged to officiate the wedding ceremony that brings the two of you together in holy matrimony!

(Author's Note – May 3, 2014 was a glorious day! What a privilege to officiate the wedding of Nicole and Dustin!!)

Seeing God At Work Every Day

"Therefore a man leaves his father and his mother and cleaves to his wife, and they become one flesh." (Genesis. 2:24 Revised Standard Version)

Take an inventory of the relationships you have. Write down a few names of people with which you have significant relationship. How does your relationship measure up with the simple rules of arithmetic?

Addition

Subtraction

Multiplication

Division

Fractions

Pray for "Healthy Relationships!!"

23

Wing Clippers

I was visiting with someone who had just had his "wings clipped."

Seeing God At Work Every Day

Ever have your wings clipped?

As much as it hurts or stings, having my wings clipped by God is understandable and always appropriate. There are times when God has to reign me in to protect me, to teach me and to show me another way of how to "fly" through life.

But then, there are other times when someone comes along in your life that is a "Wing Clipper!"

Oh how they love to politely invite you to sit down and chat with them.
They bring you into their confidence.
They are extra nice and sweet.
They charm you into trusting them.

And then... BAM!!!
Clip clip clip Clip clip clip Clip clip clip Clip clip clip Clip clip clip Clip clip clip Clip clip clip Clip clip clip Clip clip clip Clip clip clip Clip clip clip Clip clip clip Clip clip clip Clip clip clip Clip clip clip Clip clip clip Clip clip clip....

David Dendy

Before you know it...all your feathers are scattered on the floor and there you stand as powerful as an Ostrich to fly (By the way... Ostriches can't fly!)

These "Wing Clippers" love to control other people.
They are "control freaks."
Watch out for them!
They will "clip" you alive and leave you flightless, powerless and most hurtful of all...
they will leave you less than who God made you to be.

I am a firm believer that God has given us wings...
- to swoop...
- to fly...
- to flit...
- to flutter...
- to soar...

Spread you wings
Soar high today on the thermals of God's freedom, God's grace and God's love!

Seeing God At Work Every Day

"but they who wait for the Lord shall renew their strength;
they shall mount up with wings like eagles... (Isaiah 40:31 ESV)

When was the last time you had your wings clipped by someone? What were the circumstances surrounding the "clipping?" Have you ever clipped someone else's wings?

Has God ever done a little "wing clipping" on you? If so, what was the ultimate outcome?

What steps can be taken to avoid the ever controlling "Wing Clippers" in our lives?

David Dendy

When was the last time you felt like you were soaring like an eagle through life?

Provide the "wind beneath someone's wings" today and help someone soar who may have been grounded for a while...

24

God in the Box

I saw an advertisement for a movie called "God in the Box."
The premise of the movie was to ask people two very important questions...

What does God look like?

What does God mean to you?

Seeing God At Work Every Day

I would like to offer my answer to these two questions. I am feeling the pressure to come up with some incredibly profound answer that will blow the mind of each reader and have everyone walking away from this chapter shaking their head in complete and utter spiritual amazement!! Don't get your hopes up...

What does God look like?

Being the good "Trinitarian" that I am, I always think of God as three distinct, unique persons.

God the Father, God the Son and God the Holy Spirit - Three in One.

When I think of God the Father, I just see the color white. It's not a blinding brilliant white but rather a soft, warm inviting white. I see no face but I do see large, strong yet gentle hands being extended from under robed arms. Furthermore, I see knees bent at a ninety degree angle under His massive white robe as God sits on some type of throne. I see no feet but I do see myself sitting, kneeling at the feet of God.

When I think of God the Son I have a definite picture in mind of what Jesus looks like. I am positive that my mind's eye has been influenced by movies, paintings and other visual mediums. Jesus is dark skinned, long thick brown wavy hair resting on a tall, strong and lean frame. I always picture Jesus wearing a tanned colored robe. Sometimes I wonder what Jesus would look like wearing jeans. Jesus has a brilliant smile and a contagious laugh. But, it is His eyes that captivate and mesmerize my every vision. Dazzling brown with deep black pupils surrounded by soft features, it is the eyes of Jesus that draw me in more than any other physical aspect. His eyes always reflect what I need... Encouraging, supportive, loving, corrective, forgiving, humorous, accepting, life giving and full of grace. When I look into the eyes of Jesus, the rest of the world disappears.

When I think of God the Holy Spirit - I see the wind, which is to say, I see nothing and yet at the same time this wind feels like gentle hands with strong feminine characteristics, comforting and soothing to the touch of my inner being and soul. I can feel and see the effects of the Holy Spirit.

What does God mean to you?

This is indeed a tough, thought provoking question.

God means everything to me.

God is...
- the foundation on which I stand.
- the post on which I lean.
- the power that fuels my pursuits, my personality and my passions.
- my shelter, my savior and my satisfaction.

God is...

- not far away and distant but rather very personal, protective and providential.
- the comfort in which I lay myself down and peacefully rest and sleep.
- the keeper of the promises so that I can walk forward in life with full assurance and confidence.
- the warrior that stands beside me in the most conflicted situations and shouts at the top of His lungs... "Fear not David! For I am with you!!"

God is...

- the strength upon which I crumple when I finally admit just how weak and insecure I really am.
- the extended hand that I hold on to as hard as I can, only to realize that it is the hand of God that forever holds on to me even when I let go.
- the giver of all things and the only framework from which I can operate is one of gracious gratitude.

God is...

- supremely powerful and yet is surprisingly gentle with my heart.
- God is God and I am not... (one of these days I will finally grasp this...)
- the Hound of Heaven who runs after me and pursues me relentlessly when I run away and try to hide. He finds me every time!!
- the detailed planner with an incessant creative imagination whose plans, hopes and desires are "far more" than my wildest dreams could possibly imagine.

God is...

- the One, the only one who understands and accepts everything about me.
- the One with whom I find great delight, joy and extreme laughter which in turn makes me "laugh often."

- the One who offers me hope in the most hopeless of situations, love when I am most unlovable and acceptance when I am most unacceptable.

God is...
- the Voice that proclaims, "You are forgiven!" over and over and over and over and over and over and over and over....
- the hands that wrap around my face as His loving thumbs wipe away my every tear and whispers in my ear... "I understand..."
- the elbow in my ribs as He says, "Hey David... check this out." And I do and I then stand there in utter amazement.
- the great Memory Bank who reminds me who I am and whose I am when I forget.

God is...
- the unconditional love that melts my heart each and every day.
- my all in all.
- the tape at the finish line that patiently waits to enfold me as I run the race of life, stumbling and crawling across the line exhausted and exhilarated!

God is...
- the One who waits on the 50 yard line of the stadium of heaven in the presence of the great cloud of witnesses and announces to the sold out crowd, "Ladies and Gentleman, boys and girls, from Houston, Texas, a child of the covenant, a son of the King - David Wilkes Dendy", as I come running through the tunnel out on to the heavenly field and jump into the everlasting arms of Jesus to the deafening applause of heaven!

That's what God means to me...

Seeing God At Work Every Day

"...because, if you confess with your mouth that Jesus is Lord and believe in your heart that God raised him from the dead, you will be saved. For with the heart one believes and is justified, and with the mouth one confesses and is saved." (Romans 10:9-10 ESV)

Now it's your turn...

What does God look like?

What does God mean to you?

25

Hello! My Name Is...

At a recent gathering I had the privilege of introducing myself to someone. What rolled off my tongue is what has rolled off my tongue for the last 35 plus years...

"Hello! My Name Is David Dendy..."

Seeing God At Work Every Day

This has been my protocol for over 35 years.
I have introduced myself to tens of thousands of people in this very manner...
There have been a few stark variations over the years...

1. Hi, my name is David Dendy...
2. Hey, my name is David Dendy...
3. Hey, I'm David Dendy...
4. I am David Dendy...
5. I'm David Dendy...
6. By the way... my name is David Dendy

You get the picture.

Do you know where this little insecure idiosyncrasy comes from?
Of course you don't!

I am about to tell you.

Back in the days of rotary dial phones when caller ID was but a cartoon reality on "The Jetsons," I had a "puppy dog" type crush on a girl. I couldn't have been more than 14 years of age. After deliberating with myself for over an hour in getting up the courageous nerve to call her, I finally, yet reluctantly, placed my right index finger in the rotary dial and performed a series of short staccato clockwise movements that in effect "dialed" her number. I had rehearsed my opening line to perfection.

When the phone was finally answered, I heard her very familiar voice on the other end of the line. With bold insecure confidence I said, "Hi insert girl's name here! This is David." (That was my opening line!)

The silence on the other end of the phone was deafening...
The pregnant pause was interminable...
Beads of sweat spontaneously popped up all over my forehead...
My mind was racing...

And then she spoke these unforgettable words...

"David who?"

Only seven words had been spoken and the conversation was already over.

You see... the reason I say, *"Hi, My name is David Dendy"*, is that there is a huge part of me that truly believes that you will forget who I am if I don't tell you my whole name.

I have been forgotten in the past and it is a terrible feeling.
I don't want to be forgotten again.

That's why it is so important for me to call people by their name.
I figure since I love nothing more than hearing my name called, I will return the favor to those around me...

Here is the good news!
God knows our name and calls us by name!

Seeing God At Work Every Day

"Fear not, for I have redeemed you;
I have called you by name, you are mine." (Isaiah 43:1 ESV)

As you have probably figured out by now, finding comfort and confidence in "knowing" that God does in fact "know" us by name is a popular theme for me and for this book.

Do you every feel like people "forget" who you are? How does that make you feel?

Work hard today to call people by name (the grocery clerk, coworkers, receptionists, your family!) and see what a difference it makes.

Say your own name out loud several times today...

26

The Ordinary Trucker

I parked my car in the University parking lot where I always park.

Right in front of me an 18 wheeler pulled up and parked on the side of the street with the top of his tractor trailer intimately kissing the branches of about three trees.

I got out.
The trucker with furry eyebrows got out.
I walked around my car with my blazer, blue tie and khaki pants.
He walked around his idling truck with his well-worn jeans and long untucked T-shirt.
I looked at him.
He looked at me through his silver rimmed glasses while he "hand combed" his scraggly hair out of the way of his view.
He said, *"Excuse me, but I understand that there is a new building going up around here. Do you know where it might be?"*
I thought to myself, *"A man, a man asking for directions!"*

What ensued was a most pleasant 15 minute conversation about trucking, his family that lives in Denver, his son who works in the sheriff's department in Greeley, Colorado, the devastation of the recent flooding in Colorado, the potential hazards of getting stuck in the snow, his trucking company, his 18 wheeler cab that has a microwave, refrigerator, ten gallons of water and a great bed and yes, we ultimately talked about where the new building was and how to get there.

He told me his name was Clinton Nicholas.
I told him my name was David Dendy (of course I did...)

We shook hands.
I told him to be safe out on the road and *"God Bless..."*
And into his truck went "The Ordinary Trucker."

Seeing God At Work Every Day

Nothing spectacular...
Nothing really out of the ordinary...
Nothing that will make you rethink your position on race relations, current politics, the deity of Christ or the rise and fall of the local economy...
Nothing but a friendly conversation among two men that just happened to meet.

And this is what I find extraordinary...
God being found in the ordinary.

Perhaps I need to look there more often to see and experience the wonder of our awesome God.
How about you?
Where will you discover God today?
What may seem as "ordinary" just might be the most extraordinary display of our creator God...

Seeing God At Work Every Day

"The Lord said, "Go out and stand on the
mountain in the presence of the Lord,
for the Lord is about to pass by." Then a great and powerful wind
tore the mountains apart and shattered the rocks before the Lord,
but the Lord was not in the wind. After the wind there was an
earthquake, but the Lord was not in the earthquake. After the
earthquake came a fire, but the Lord was not in the fire. And after
the fire came a still small voice." (1 Kings 19:11-13 NIV)

Think of a time where God showed up in an extraordinary way through a most ordinary event...

Reflect on the Bible verse above where God actually showed up in a "still small voice." Does that seem out of character for the God you have come to know?

Look for God in the ordinary and perhaps mundane events of today and record them here...

27

51 minutes...

Have you ever wondered if your life is making a difference?

My son's second grade teacher had a granddaughter born on Monday, September 23rd.
Listen to this announcement in our local newspaper on Thursday, September 26th...

Savannah Jane Houselog, baby daughter of Andy and Beth Houselog, of Dubuque, was taken into eternal happiness at 9:45 a.m. on Monday, September 23, 2013, after gracing the world with her presence for 51 minutes.

Seeing God At Work Every Day

I was getting dressed for work and Julie dropped the obituary section of the paper on my lap and said, *"If you want a really good cry, read this."* I read the opening paragraph and started to gasp for my breath as tears overfilled my eyes and began racing down my cheek finding the finish line at my chin.

The obituary went on to explain that at the routine 20 week ultrasound checkup some medical complications were noticed and explained to Andy and Beth that should this baby go to full term the likely outcome would be a very short life. Andy and Beth decided to go full term. Along the way they took Savannah to a Red Sox game, a hot air balloon ride, motorcycle, boat and hayrides. Evidently, Savannah loved DQ blizzards, Dove chocolates, and adored the voices of her big sister and big brother reading to her as she would kick her legs in delight. She used to kick so much that the older sister nicknamed Savannah, *"Bumblebee."*

Savannah changed the world in which she lived.
Her beautiful face, her soft cry and her legacy of unconditional love to her family will never be forgotten.

The obituary went on to declare the great faith of the Houselog family as they joyfully shared how Savannah was greeted at heaven's gates by her big sister Sylvia and her great grandparents.

The obituary ended with these words of incredible perspective...

"We would rather have
had one breath of her hair,
one kiss of her mouth,
one touch of her hand,
than an eternity without it."

Let me close with the same question I opened with...

"Have you ever wondered if your life is making a difference?"

Whether you have been alive for...
51 years
51 months
51 days
or even
51 minutes...

The answer is a definite, "YES!"
If no one has told you lately, then let me have the honors...

God has knitted you together with great care and with greater love.
The way your eyes smile,

101

David Dendy

The tenderness of your touch,
The uniqueness of your voice,
The strength of your hugs,
The creativity of your mind,
The love of your heart,
The humor of your laughter,
Oh dear child of God...
I would rather have a moment of any of those things,
than an eternity without it...

Seeing God At Work Every Day

"So teach us to number our days that we may get
a heart of wisdom." (Psalm 90:12 ESV)

Have you ever wondered if your life is making a difference?

Psalm 90 encourages us to "number our days that we may get a heart of wisdom." In what ways are you numbering your days to make each day count?

Take a moment to offer a prayer for the Houselog family...

Take a moment to reach out to those you know that have lost a child or a loved one at such a young age...

And now... take a moment to reflect on this:

God has knitted you together with great care and with greater love.
The way your eyes smile,
The tenderness of your touch,
The uniqueness of your voice,
The strength of your hugs,

David Dendy

The creativity of your mind,
The love of your heart,
The humor of your laughter,
Oh dear child of God...
I would rather have a moment of any of those things,
than an eternity without it...

28

Labels

Does the number **24601** spark any particular feelings, memories or remembrances?

At first glance that number reminds me of the childhood cheer we used to say after Little League games... "2 4 6 8 who do we appreciate... (then yell the opposing team's name)?" Perhaps it's the population of a town nearby. Maybe it's a statistic that represents the number of people who bought iPhones in the last hour...

Or maybe it's a *__Label...__*

For Jean Valjean in the play/movie Les Miserables it is his prison number. In prison Jean Valjean has no name, no identity, and no sense of personhood. For nineteen winters strong his captor, his corrections officer, his personal nemesis and pursuer Javert has called Jean Valjean not by his God given name but rather by this number... this label.

Then Jean Valjean is set free and then breaks parole. Soon he has an incredible redemptive encounter and becomes a successful businessman, a strong, caring, loving and faithful follower and practitioner of the Christian faith. His life changes in all ways.

But not in the eyes of Javert. Jean Valjean is still prisoner **24601** and Javert pursues him for year upon year as Prisoner 24601 who broke parole and who has not changed, who cannot change, who will not change. After all, you are what you are and you can never change.

Seeing God At Work Every Day

What label do you carry around?

What label hangs around your neck? What label have you allowed yourself or others to tattoo on your forehead? Athlete? Nerd? Neat freak? Overweight? Obsessive Compulsive? Loser? Divorced? Single? Adulterer? Lakers fan? Workaholic? Alcoholic? Successful? Type A personality? The list could go on and on.

What is sad about labels is that over time we learn to accept them. The label becomes the lens in which we see ourselves. Although the "bling" on these labels has tarnished and spoiled we continue to wear them and try to polish them and live with them and dress them up because after all I am what I am and I can never change.

Is that what we believe? Is this what we practice? Is this how we live out our lives?

The scriptures tell us that in Christ, We are a new creation! "The old has passed away; behold, the new has come... For freedom Christ has set us free..." (2 Corinthians 5:17 ESV and Galatians 5:1 ESV)

In Christ the labels slip off! In Christ you are free! Free! Do we even begin to understand what that means? I wonder myself sometimes...

We have been made new! We don't have to stand where we have fallen, we can step forward out of yesterday's shadow.

In Christ, here are some new labels that never tarnish, never fade...

- *Child of God,*
- *Son and Daughter of the King,*
- *Forgiven,*
- *Freed,*
- *Redeemed,*
- *Saved,*
- *Loved,*
- *Accepted...*

In Christ we are no longer a number or a label. We have been claimed and redeemed by name.

"'Fear not! For I have redeemed you; I have called you by name. You are mine,' says the Lord." (Isaiah 43:1 ESV)

And perhaps this is the best label of all... **I am the Lord's**

Seeing God At Work Every Day

"Fear not! For I have redeemed you;
I have called you by name. You are mine," says the Lord.
(Isaiah 43:1 ESV)

What labels do you carry around that weigh you down?

What would it take to shed some of those labels that keep you from soaring?

What does the label "I am the Lord's" mean to you?

Challenge yourself today to put an end to placing labels around the necks of those around us…

29

Nine More Minutes...

He's fifty-nine years old and in those fifty-nine years he has taken more abuse than anyone I have ever met. He's been hit at least once or twice a day and yet for some reason he stays close by the one who hits him the most.

Most of us, at first observation would say, *"Move out of harm's way!!"* And yet, he has decided to stay near the hand that hits him on a daily basis, his master's hand having some sort of hypnotic power over his inability to move away and seek shelter.

Is he loyal?
To a fault...
Is he stupid?
I wouldn't go that far... He really believes that he is providing a valuable service to his master.
Will he seek therapy?
I sincerely doubt it. He's a prisoner in his own home.
Does he work?
Mostly in the mornings. He has a great "bedside manner."
What's his name?
Telechron 7H241... better known as "The Snooze Button."

Thanks to the General Electric Company, the "Telechron 7H241" was unveiled in 1956 as the *"most humane alarm clock ever invented."* And for the last fifty-nine years we have been hitting Mr. Telechron 7H241 every day since!

My personal record for hitting the Snooze Button is fourteen times in a row. The Snooze Button is the only device ever invented that helps us enjoy doing math in our head.

For example, the alarm goes off and you have one hour to get ready. Hit the snooze and your brain immediately does the math and you determine you can do an hour's worth of getting ready in fifty-one minutes.

Boom!! Nine minutes later you hit Mr. Telechron 7H241 again and the mental math gymnastics continues, *"I know I can get it all done in forty-two!"* (And then your mind starts to race... "42? Oh, that was a great movie... Jackie Robinson.... Jackie? My friend who lives in Iowa...Iowa? Corn... I love corn and how I eat it like a typewriter...Typewriter? I loved learning how to type on the manual Olympic... Olympics? I am stepping up to the starting line for the 100 meter dash, the starter raises his gun and BOOM!...)

The Alarm has gone off again and now you have thirty-three minutes and you are up and at 'em all mad because, He, Mr. Telechron 7H241 ruined your morning by getting you off to a late start.
Off to work you go, vowing that you will get revenge on Mr. Telechron 7H241 tomorrow morning!
And you do...just to get nine more minutes...

Seeing God At Work Every Day

Well... that was kind of silly wasn't it?

But, oh so true!
I wonder how many times God offers an alarm, a wakeup call to us.
Only to have us lie there...
Offer a big heavy sigh...
Roll over...
Roll our eyes...

And in one quick motion that belies our current state we smack the Snooze Button.
To return to our dreams
To rest in our sleepy, non-productive state of being
To ignore the call to action
To put off for nine more minutes the inevitable
To delay the potential joy of a renewed sense of communion with the Holy of Holies...

There are lots of studies out there that show that the repeated abuse of the Telecrhon 7H241 is actually bad for your body and your health.

There are lots of scriptures out there that show the repeated abuse of putting God off for "later" is actually bad for our spiritual health.

What would happen if we actually "woke up", "got up" and "listened up" on the first call?

Hold on...
Excuse me for just a minute...
My alarm just went off...
BOOM...
I'll get back to you later...
Please give me just nine more minutes...

Seeing God At Work Every Day

"And the Lord came and stood, calling as at other times, 'Samuel! Samuel!' And Samuel said, 'Speak, for your servant hears.'" (1 Samuel 3:10 ESV)

Has God ever called you to do something and without really thinking about it, you hit the "snooze" button and went back to slumber land?

What are some of the actions that God is calling you to do today? Will you jump at the opportunity or will you hit the "snooze" button?

What makes you hit the "snooze" button time and time again?

Reflect on what life would look like today if you responded right away to God's call...

30

Guilt, Shame and Vulnerability

Wow! This is going to be fun chapter to read!!
What a great way to start my day! Thanks David!!

Many of our lives seem to be heavily influenced by these three words.
Guilt...Shame...Vulnerability...

How about yours?

Guilt - feeling remorseful about a recognized wrong doing toward one's self or another oftentimes framed as, *"I made a mistake."*

Shame - an internalized feeling of negative self-reflection oftentimes framed as, *"I am a mistake.* Branding our self with phrases such as *"I'm not good enough"* and *"I'm not worthy enough"* also apply.

Vulnerable - the courage to open one's self to those around us in a way that is completely honest, totally authentic, with no pretense and no pretending that oftentimes leads to the heartbeat of creativity, innovation and change, oftentimes framed as, *"I am going out on a limb here..."*

Seeing God At Work Every Day

When do you feel most alive?

What activity do you participate in where you feel God's pleasure?

When do you feel most vulnerable?

I am going to go out on a limb here and propose that when we are the most vulnerable, it is then that we feel most alive, most energized, most aware, and most afraid. All five senses are in full overdrive and our pulse quickens and our mind races like a Formula One driver.

What keeps us from being vulnerable?
More than likely the culture that surrounds us identifies "vulnerability" with "weakness."

Hogwash!!! (That's the nicest way for me to put it...)

Have you ever witnessed someone be totally vulnerable?
What word comes to mind when you observe this?

I don't know about you, but "courage" is what comes to my mind.
Then, why are we so unwilling to be vulnerable?
Because we are weak!

Do you know what happens when we are not vulnerable?
We become *"strong"* which then leads to *"secrecy"* because we don't want anyone to know just how *"weak"* we really are and *"secrecy"* leads to a whole host of dysfunctional, disillusioned deficiencies that leave us weakened, bitter, adamant, tight fisted, stiff necked control freaks fueled by an incredible sense of shame.

Do you know who stopped this crazy circle and cycle of life by going out on a limb, literally?

Jesus...

And He can help you stop yours too...
I know He has helped me stop mine...

Seeing God At Work Every Day

"And being found in human form, he humbled himself by
becoming obedient to the point of death, even death on a cross.
Therefore God has highly exalted him and bestowed on him
the name that is above every name, so that at the name of Jesus
every knee should bow, in heaven and on earth and under the
earth, and every tongue confess that Jesus Christ is Lord,
to the glory of God the Father."(Philippians 2:8-11 ESV)

What emotions and/or feelings come to mind when you start reflecting on
guilt, shame and vulnerability?

Do you currently reside in a family or workplace that encourages
vulnerability? Have you ever felt the freedom to be vulnerable with someone?

In your prayers today, be vulnerable with God by emptying yourself before Him...

What would it take to be vulnerable with a close friend or family member?

Reread this classic verse above from Paul's letter to the Philippians and reflect on how vulnerable Jesus is in this description...

31

Full Acceptance

I received an email from a friend of mine that prompted this memory...

Many years ago, perhaps when I was in Junior High school, some family friends of ours were going through the adoption process. During one of the interviews by the adoption agency, the father, in order to assess his readiness to be a father, was asked the following hypothetical question, *"If your daughter came home pregnant, what would you do?"*

His answer has stuck with me all these years...
"I would love her..."

Seeing God At Work Every Day

Pick the situation that applies to you...

Your son or daughter comes home and says...

1. I am pregnant...
2. I am marrying a person of a different race...
3. I am dating a person of a different faith or religion...
4. I have a venereal disease...
5. I am moving out...
6. I am addicted to pornography...

7. I am an alcoholic...
8. I am depressed...
9. I am a homosexual...
10. I am a woman trapped in a man's body...
11. I have just accepted Jesus as my Lord and Savior
12. I just shot someone...
13. I just lost my job...
14. I hate you...
15. I am getting divorced

My friend that emailed me yesterday shared with me that their child had come home and shared one of those fifteen statements listed above...

Do you know what my friend's response was to their child?
Well, here... let me let you read it for yourself...

"I love you!
I will support you no matter what!
You will lose family and you will lose friends, but not here.
Not from me..."

The love of a mom and/or a dad can be unconditional and one of full acceptance.
Notice I said, "can be."
Sadly, sometimes a parent's love is not unconditional and not one of full acceptance.

Here's the good news...
Hear the good news...

Our heavenly Father's love "is" unconditional and one of full acceptance!
Whatever we are carrying around...
Whatever is weighing us down...
Whatever we need to get off of our chest...
Whatever we are running from...
The Father runs to us and holds us close with words and actions of "full acceptance."

His words are this: *I love you! No matter what!*

PS - My friend is a faithful reader of this book.
To my dear and faithful friend,
please hear these words from me...
"I love you!
I will support you no matter what!
You will lose family and you will lose friends,
but not here.
Not from me..."

Seeing God At Work Every Day

And Jesus said, "All that the Father gives me will come to me,
and whoever comes to me I will never cast out." (John 6:37 ESV)
"Let us then with confidence draw near to the throne of grace,
that we may receive mercy and find grace to help
in time of need." (Hebrews 4:16 ESV)

If someone very close to you confesses to you one of the above 15 statements would you be able to accept them completely? Why or why not?

Who are the people in your life that say to you, *"I love you! I will support you no matter what! You will lose family and you will lose friends, but not here. Not from me…!"*

Who are the people in your life that rely on you to love them and support them no matter what?

Thank God for family and friends who support us and accept us completely and fully!!

32

Held for Ransom

We are all creatures of habit.
Never was this truer than at the First Presbyterian Church in Klamath Falls, Oregon where I used to serve as the pastor.

When I preached, I would look out over the congregation and lo and behold everyone who came to church sat in the same place every Sunday. In the back right was this family and in the front left another certain family occupied the same pew every Sunday.

Kris Ransom was no different.

On the Sundays that she was able to make it, Kris would take the side aisle nearest to the entry door and walk past twelve or thirteen pews, make a right hand turn and scoot over to about halfway across the selected pew. There she sat in the third or fourth pew from the front with the brightest smile on her face, her countenance brilliantly lighting up the front of the church. As a preacher, I always appreciated it when people would actually look at me when I preached. I loved catching people's eyes during the sermon and my eyes would twinkle at catching the sparkling eyes of Kris Ransom. The fact that she was suffering from breast cancer did not define who she was. Who she was worshiping is what defined Kris Ransom.

David Dendy

Like many others who have fought the fight of cancer, the beast of breast cancer finally won the battle over Kris' body after a 25 year struggle.

Seeing God At Work Every Day

I wasn't there for the end of Kris' life but I have a feeling that those sparkling eyes and brilliant smile never faded, never stopped and never ceased even though her body was getting ready to.

Here's my take on why her face and her mind and her heart would take on such a posture right up to the very end.

This is what I believe Kris envisioned was ahead of her during this last week of her life.

The day was going to come when she would shed this shell of a human body and be escorted to the peaceful place of perpetual paradise. As she would glide toward the heavenly gates she would meet Jesus face to face and they would embrace. And Jesus would lean back and say, *"Before I let you in Kris we have to go through a bit of a formality. Let me open the Book of Life and let me see if your name is in it."*

Jesus flips through the pages of this ginormous bound book and then He stops and with His right index finger He slides his hand down the page on the right hand side of the big book and suddenly His hand stops, perfectly placed over her name. Jesus looks up at Kris and says, *"Here we are. Yes! We have a spot 'held for Ransom'!"*

And Kris flashed her brilliant smile...
And Kris' twinkling eyes sparkled...

And so they did...
And now...
So they do...
Forever and ever and ever...

Seeing God At Work Every Day

"He will wipe away every tear from their eyes, and death shall be no more, neither shall there be mourning, nor crying, nor pain anymore, for the former things have passed away." (Revelation 21:4 ESV)

Do your eyes sparkle at the thought of what the future holds for you after this life has passed?

Read Revelation 21:1-4. How does this passage impact you?

Is there anyone in your life that you could pass on this assurance to who is going through a very difficult time?

May the assurance of this great passage from Revelation 21 be of great comfort and assurance for you...

33

Belly Buttons

I have the complete utter and hysterical joy of teaching fourth and fifth graders in Sunday School at my church about once or twice a month.

One particular Sunday we were going over the creation story.

"In the beginning God..." (What else do you need to know?)

We went over what God created on each day and how God just said, *"Let there be..."* and there it came to be! The power of God's word... Wow!

We went over the creation of Adam and Eve and we talked about ribs and whether or not men have fewer ribs than women because Eve was made out of Adam's rib.

We came to the end of our class time and I huddled the class together and said,

"If you only remember one thing from today, remember this...Adam and Eve didn't have belly buttons!!"

They all huffed and laughed and their jaws dropped to the floors while their eyes bugged out. *"What do you mean Mr. David that Adam and Eve didn't have belly buttons?"*

With a big serious smile on my face I explained, *"Since Adam and Eve were created from scratch they didn't have any umbilical cords."*

One of the boys interrupted me with a very quizzical look on his face...

"If they didn't have umbilical cords, how... how did they talk?"

Seeing God At Work Every Day

This little boy learned real quickly that there is a huge difference between umbilical cords and vocal cords.

Belly Buttons are great reminders that we were once connected in such a dependent way to a life source for about nine months to get our very lives up and running. Without umbilical cords we would never have come to be who we are today.

What would serve as the Belly Button for you as a vivid reminder that you are connected to the Life Source of the universe?

Perhaps it is the cross that reminds you of God's love and the ultimate sacrifice Jesus made on your behalf so that you could have life and life eternal.

Perhaps it is the Lord's Table at the church you attend and you see the powerful ancient words inscribed on the side - *"Do This In Remembrance of Me"* that draws you to the Irresistible Inviter of the Banquet Table.

Perhaps it is the ever so familiar tune and words to great songs like *"Amazing Grace"* or *"Jesus Christ is Risen Today"* that ascends your mind and heart to the music stand of the Great Conductor.

Perhaps it is the rising or the setting of the sun each day that reminds you that you are connected to the Creative Creator.

Perhaps it is a thousand other things that remind you that you are not alone but that you are connected to the One who is above all, in all and is all.

So go ahead...
Take a peek...
Stare at your belly button...
Remember to give thanks to the God who gives us life and life abundantly!

Seeing God At Work Every Day

So God created man in his own image, in the image of God he created him; male and female he created them. (Genesis 1:27 ESV)

What would serve as the Belly Button for you as a vivid reminder that you are connected to the Life Source of the universe?

Look around today and write down what you discover that reminds you of the connection you have with God.

34

Numb the Pain

Have you ever had any type of surgery?
In November of 2013 I went under "the knife" to repair an umbilical hernia.
In order to enjoy the surgery more thoroughly I was put under with general anesthesia.
The anesthesia allows me to *"sleep"* through the surgery so that the surgeon can cut me *"wide open"* and I will lie there unaffected.

Anesthesia numbs the pain. (Praise God!!!)

Seeing God At Work Every Day

When we face painful situations what do we do or use to "numb the pain?"

Or do we use anything at all to "numb the pain?"

I have known people who have used alcohol to numb the pain.
I have known people who have used drugs, legal and otherwise to numb the pain.
I have known people who have used exercise to numb the pain.
I have known people who have used excessive counseling to numb the pain.
I have known people who have used the church to numb the pain.
I have known people who have used Facebook to numb the pain.
This list could go on and on.

I think you get the point.

What about me?
What about you?
There are lots of things we can do and use to *"numb the pain."*

God is the only One who can take the pain away.
We are so quick to want to turn and run away from pain that sometimes God can't use the pain or the hurt to heal us because we numb ourselves so quickly with other substitutes. The ultimate result being, the origin of the pain is never healed and we, in a very real way "sleep" through life.

Feeling some pain today?
Let's not be so quick to "numb the pain" with self-manufactured anesthesia. What would happen if we embraced the pain in its totality today and let the Divine Surgeon heal us, repair us and fix us on His own operating table of love, mercy and grace?

David Dendy

Seeing God At Work Every Day

Have mercy on me, O God, according to your steadfast love;
according to your abundant mercy blot out my transgressions.
Wash me thoroughly from my iniquity, and cleanse
me from my sin! (Psalm 51:1-2 ESV)

What have you traditionally used to "numb the pain?"

How does the idea of "embracing the pain" in its totality strike you?

Resist the urge today to quickly "numb the pain" with self-manufactured doses of self-help remedies that only prolong the pain. Instead, place the pain in the confident hands of the Divine Surgeon...

35

Fangirling

I was hanging out with my addictive friend "Facebook" and a posting from one of my smartest college classmates Lauren popped up. I read it with great interest because it contained a word that I had never heard of before.

I wouldn't have made it through college without Lauren. She was responsible for typing all of my college term papers and for cutting my hair during my four years at Davidson College. (Just to be clear... I wrote the papers, Lauren typed them... back when we used to have these contraptions called typewriters.) On her Facebook page Lauren mentioned her daughter was freaking out because the band "One Direction" had a new album coming out and that some of the songs had been "leaked." It was the last sentence of her post that caught my attention...

"Let the fangirling begin."

Fangirling? I had never hear of such a word. I was quick to jump on dictionary.com and to the best of their knowledge no such word exists in the English language. I put my *"cool, suave and debonair"* factor aside and just went straight to the source. I wrote on Lauren's Facebook page, please enlighten me to the meaning of the word *"fangirling."*

Within minutes I had my answer...

David Dendy

Urban Dictionary says:

v. 1. the reaction a fangirl has to any mention or sighting of the object of her "affection". These reactions include shortness of breath, fainting, high-pitched noises, shaking, fierce head shaking as if in the midst of a seizure, endless blog posts, etc.

2. a gathering of two or more fangirls in which they proceed to waste endless amounts of time ogling, discussing/arguing, stalking, etc. the object of their "affection"

Who knew?

Seeing God At Work Every Day

This word, *"fangirling"* got me thinking about Jesus.

Did Jesus have fans that were girls?

I'm thinking Martha was a *"fangirl."*

Jesus knocks on the door of the home of the sisters, Mary and Martha. Martha looks through the peephole and the *fangirling* begins!

"Oh Mary! Oh Mary! OMG Mary! It's Jesus! He's at the front door! What do I do?... just look at me, I am a wreck, quick get the water on the fire, I have to make him his favorite kosher meal,... hold on a minute... you get the door... I will text Lazarus... "JC @ frnt dor"... Get him to sit down in the front room... I have to make dinner... I have got to tweet this... "#Jesusnmyhouse"... get me a paper bag so I can stop hyperventilating... I have to fix my hair so I can "snapchat" us...Wait until I post a selfie with me and Jesus on Facebook! My friends are going to go crazy! I have the hottest looking chiseled six pack abs carpenter turned rabbi turned savior in my house! Woohoo!!" My blog is going to get a record number of page views today!!" "@marthastewart...I was Martha first!"

And then the *"Fangirling"* takes a nasty turn with an obsessive Martha chastising Mary to get her rear in gear and get in the kitchen and help out as Mary just sits there at the feet of Jesus.

Jesus stops all the fangirling in a heartbeat with two sentences... "Martha, Martha, you are anxious and troubled about many things, but one thing is necessary. Mary has chosen the good portion, which will not be taken away from her." (Luke 10:41-42 ESV)

I can't tell you how many "Marthas" I have run into who defend Martha by saying, "Well, someone had to get the work done."

Listen again to the words of Jesus... "Martha you are anxious and troubled about many things..."

There is nothing wrong with being a "fangirl"!

However, when being a fangirl or a fanboy leads to "anxiety" and "troubledness" then we have a problem.
That's the problem with fangirling or fanboying in the Christian world...
It treats the object of our affection, Jesus as just that... An object!
Jesus is not an object.
He is the subject of our service, our servitude and our sensibilities.
He is our Savior.
And if I can keep that in mind then...

Let the fangirling begin!

Seeing God At Work Every Day

"Martha, Martha, you are anxious and troubled about many things, but one thing is necessary. Mary has chosen the good portion, which will not be taken away from her." (Luke 10:41-42 ESV)

The Bible also says that, "Martha was distracted with much serving…" (Luke 10. 40 ESV) Have you ever been "distracted" with much serving where the service becomes the object of your affection (fangirling) rather than the service being the subject of who you are serving?

Today, choose the good portion that Mary chose and sit at the feet of Jesus today and let someone else do the chores!

Sitting at the feet of Jesus, what would you say to him? What do you think He would say to you?

36

Butterfly

At 9:45 am on a November day my dear and very close friend and fellow tennis playing partner Howard Newman walked up to the gates of heaven and received a thunderous applause and ovation as he was tenderly and ferociously received into the waiting and loving arms of Jesus.

Seeing God At Work Every Day

Many times "cancer" wins the battle...
But faith in Christ always wins the war.
Howard won the war yesterday.

As his son Greg and I were texting back and forth in the last days.
Greg offered an analogy that a friend had made... *"It is much like a caterpillar metamorphosis into a butterfly. Painful but fruitful in the end. Dad is giving birth to his spirit."*

Upon reading that text the word "butterfly" stood out and prompted this memory.

When I was in college one of my professors told us about several words in our English language that were composed of two words that somehow over the years the two words had been "flip flopped."

She gave a few examples of this strange phenomenon, but the only word that I remember is "Butterfly."

When she mentioned the word I thought to myself, *"Flip flopping those two words would give us 'fly butter.'"* As if reading my mind the professor said, *"Many of you may be thinking that 'fly butter' makes no sense."* I nodded my head in enthusiastic agreement.

She further explained, *"Think of it this way...'**flutter by.**'"*

My mind exploded in the "aha ness" of the moment!

In a very real way we *"flutter by"* on this earth.
With each flap of our delicate wings...
With each soft touching down on a flower to replenish or to rest...
With each gentle "take off"...
With each flight, dancing to the music of the sky...
We make a difference in this world.
Howard made a huge impact on my life as he "fluttered by".
May we return the favor to those we love, adore and cherish...

I love you Howard...
Thank you for loving me!

Seeing God At Work Every Day

"And do not be grieved, for the joy of the Lord is
your strength." (Nehemiah 8:10 ESV)

Name a few of the people who have "fluttered by" in your life and have made
a huge impact on your life.

In what ways are you "fluttering by" in other people's lives making an impact
on them?

Thank God today for all the people who have made a powerful impact on
your life by "fluttering by"...

37

Unsubscribe

During the festive season of Black Friday and Cyber Monday, I have received hundreds of emails from mortgage companies wanting to slash my payments, investment firms telling me where to invest my money, internet outlets sharing where the greatest bargains in the history of shopping can be found and car dealerships tempting me to buy $30,000 automobiles.

I cannot for the life of me figure out what I bought online that would have triggered all these websites trying to secure my money, my attention, my life, my business, my family, my dog... well, you get the picture.

I have noticed one interesting thing about all of these offers. At the bottom of each message, in very small print comes their best offer in just one word - **Unsubscribe**.

And with a couple of extra keystrokes... I do!

Seeing God At Work Every Day

I wonder what would happen if we took an extensive inventory of the things which clutter and vie for our attention on an everyday basis.

How many items, voices, people, thoughts, offers would that inventory list?

Of those items which ones do we need to **Unsubscribe**?

What would happen if we filtered out those things which simply and profoundly distract us from being focused on the main thing in our life? Of course that raises a very pertinent and poignant question...What is the main thing in my life?

Every offer that demands our attention, time and being comes with an **Unsubscribe** button. Take the time necessary to punch it.

Give yourself an early Christmas present...

Click the **Unsubscribe** button...

It just might be the best gift you ever receive...

Seeing God At Work Every Day

Turn my eyes from looking at worthless things;
and give me life in your ways. (Psalm 119:37 ESV)

What are some of the things and/or people that you need to unsubscribe from?

What is the main thing in life? How can you become more focused on it?

Spend time today making a list of those things that will allow you to stay more focused on the "main thing" in life…

38

HUGS

If you don't like reading politically "incorrect" statements or suggestions please stop reading right now. In fact, if you stop reading right now I would love to meet you. I have never met someone who is "politically correct" all the time.

I was watching a show on TV where a counselor was trying to help reconcile two ladies. The counselor kept saying to the one lady, *"Hug her! Give her a hug! Go on... Hug her."*

The one lady was hesitant and did not want to hug the other lady.

The counselor in a very strong, firm, yet gentle, loving voice said, "Hug her. Hugs stand for **H**elping **U**s **G**row **S**piritually."

Helping
Us
Grow
Spiritually...

I love it!

David Dendy

Seeing God At Work Every Day

Here comes the politically incorrect part of the chapter.

Hug someone today.

Reach out and physically touch and embrace another human being. Don't do what I call the "Butterfly" hug where you lean over at the waist and perhaps your shoulder lightly touches another person's shoulder while you flap your hands on their back ever so gently and softly. I mean... HUG someone! Embrace them fully!

If the acronym HUGS holds true, then I was the most spiritually grown man when I was pastoring First Presbyterian Church in Klamath Falls, Oregon. I hugged about 300-400 people a week.

If the acronym HUGS holds true, then I am shriveling away spiritually in the academic, university setting. If I hug one person a week while on campus that might be stretching it just a bit. The university setting is a "no touching, no hugging zone" for the most part. For me, who loves to embrace, this has been one of the more difficult transitions.

Yes, I understand that "touching" has a very negative connotation these days with all the sexual abuse scandals that have gone on in the past decade. I get it. But, in the same sense it seems like we have thrown the baby out with the bath water. We have this incredible gift from God of "touch and feel" (one of our five senses) and with each passing day this gift gets placed high on the shelf for no one to see or touch or use.

If Jesus was around today in the flesh He would have a problem on his hands, literally.

Jesus loved to touch and embrace people.

And they were bringing children to him that he might touch them, and the disciples rebuked them. But when Jesus saw it, he was indignant and said to them, 'Let the children come to me; do not hinder them, for to such belongs the kingdom of God. Truly, I say to you, whoever does not receive the kingdom of God like a child shall not enter it.' And he took them in his arms and blessed them, laying his hands on them." (Mark 10:13-16 ESV)

There is something very spiritual,
- very healing,
- very refreshing,
- very freeing,
- very invigorating when we embrace one another.

HUGS!
Let's grow spiritually today...

Seeing God At Work Every Day

"Greet one another with a holy kiss." (Romans 16:16 ESV)
Just stick with hugging today!!

In your culture at home, work, friends and family, is hugging encouraged or discouraged?

Who was the last person you fully embraced with a hug? Why did you hug that person?

Make a list of all the people you are going to hug over the next week or two… and see if you grow spiritually.

Remember – **HUGS** – **H**elping **U**s **G**row **S**piritually

39

Superman

Faster than a speeding bullet!
More powerful than a locomotive!
Able to leap tall buildings in a single bound!

"Look, up in the sky! It's a bird! It's a plane! It's SUPERMAN!"

Yes, it's Superman, strange visitor from another planet, who came to Earth with powers and abilities far beyond those of mortal men.

Superman, who can change the course of mighty rivers, bend steel in his bare hands, and who, disguised as Clark Kent, mild mannered reporter for a great metropolitan newspaper, fights a never-ending battle for truth, justice and the American way!

You have probably figured out by now that the man in the picture above is not the Superman of the television series.

It's just my friend Tim.
Mild mannered builder/architect from Klamath Falls, Oregon.
He's not very fast. He might post a 16 second run in the 40 yard dash.
He's not very strong. Probably weighs in at less than 150 these days.
At best, his vertical leap is around 4 inches.

I love this photo of him wearing a Superman Shirt.
At the time this photo was taken he was about two hours away from having life threatening pancreatic cancer surgery.

He's in his hotel room surrounded by family.
This photo showed up on my phone.
His incredible wife Cec texted it to me at 5:00 in the morning.

As I gazed at my friend, my brother in Christ and looked at that "S" on his shirt, I wondered what that "S" might stand for:
- "Strong?"
- "Scared?"
- "Surrender?"
- "Silly?"

My phone rang 20 minutes after this photo was taken.
It was Tim's wife who is known as *"The Incredible Wife Cec"!*

Her voice was upbeat... *"Now David, we have everyone in the hotel room here (family that is). And we are going to put the phone down right in the middle of all of us and we are going to circle up around the phone and hold hands and oh, by the way you are on speaker phone and we want you to pray for us before we go to the hospital. Ok David, are you ready? We are ready for your prayer..."*

And so I prayed and I prayed and my voice was strong and then it was weak and then it quivered and then I cried as I invoked upon the name of the Lord God almighty to do a "super" miraculous healing work on a most "super man" who is a brother, a husband, a dad, a son, a father-in-law, a grandfather and a friend.

And then I said, *"And everyone said, (And together we said) "Amen!"*
There was a moment of silence as we all collected ourselves and then Tim's deep, slow, melodic voice came over the speaker... *"David, thank you..."*

And then, *"The Incredible Wife Cec"* came on and offered her thanks and her love and we hung up.
And they were off to the hospital, for surgery, to remove a cancer that has taken the life away from so many other people...

<u>Seeing God At Work Every Day</u>

I've gazed upon this picture of Tim from time to time.
My eyes always turn first to the light that seems to be coming out of his left armpit right near his heart.
The backdrop of a hotel room looks ever so familiar to me as I spent six years living in hotels from week to week as a consultant.
The two clinched fists speak volumes of the inner strength that Tim has found through our Lord and God.
His face evokes confidence and calmness in the midst of life's greatest storm.

And then there is the "S"...
What does that "S" stand for?

Here's my take...
- Surrounded by a loving family...
- Secure in the loving knowledge that he is in the hollow of God's hand and God never lets go!
- Saved by the blood of Jesus Christ who loves Tim more than Tim will ever know.
- Serene - Jesus is able to give us a sense of peace that passes all understanding.

147

- **Strong** - When we are weak, God makes us strong. I know that that is an oxymoron and rather paradoxical, but all I can say at the moment is that Tim is at his strongest right now.

Last but not least...
Superman!

Tim is a super man because of a Super Man who came into this world about 2,000 years ago with powers and abilities far beyond those of mortal men. A man who changed the course of history, bent the most bent out of shape people back into shape, loved the unlovable, spared the condemned and fights a never ending battle for the way, the truth and the life so that we may enjoy life and life eternal.

I don't know about you, but I think that is Super!

ps - A week out of from the above photo there are two more words that come to mind when I look at the letter **"S"**...

"Surgery...Successful!!!!"

Seeing God At Work Every Day

"But he (Jesus) said to me, 'My grace is sufficient
for you, for my power is made
perfect in weakness.' Therefore I will boast all
the more gladly of my weaknesses,
so that the power of Christ may rest upon me. For the sake of Christ, then,
I am content with weaknesses, insults, hardships,
persecutions, and calamities.
For when I am weak, then I am strong." (2 Corinthians 12:9-10 ESV)

What is your understanding of this most paradoxical phrase... "For when I am weak, then I am strong?"

Think of a time in your life where you were weak and yet at the same time felt very strong in Christ...

Do you know of anyone going through an upcoming surgery, chemotherapy or some other medical procedure? Take time to pray for them, their families, the doctors, the nurses...

40

Never Gives Up...

I picked up Faith and Joshua from "Kid's Club", our church's Wednesday night program for kids.

In the crowded parking lot I grabbed their hands, Faith on the left, Joshua on the right as a cacophony of red brake lights and white reverse lights lit up the sky. I couldn't quite locate my sedan in the jungle of mini-vans and Joshua loudly wondered, *"How can you not know where you parked?"*

Safely in the car with seat belts buckled we were on our way home and that's when this deep theological discussion took place.

Dad: What did y'all learn about tonight?
Children: Awwww, uhhhhh, well, well...
Dad: You don't remember?
Children: Nooooooooooooooooooooooo
Faith: The story about the lost son.
Dad: The Prodigal Son?
Joshua: Yes, the son was lost but then he returned home and his father came running to him.
Dad: What does that story say about God?
Joshua: That He will never give up on you...

Seeing God At Work Every Day

Never gives up...

That is really good news for us.
God never gives up on us.

Our co-workers will...
Our community will...
Our insurance companies will...
Our Facebook friends will...
Our "exes" will...
Our friends will...
Our enemies already have...
Even our own families will...
We may even give up on our self...

I am ashamed to admit that there have been a few people in my life and travels that I have given up on.

For many of us whether it be through
hurt or hurdles,
emotional beatings or betrayals,
nonsensical negativity or neglect,
flat out meanness or madness,
we simply do not have the capacity to keep getting slapped in the face by the proverbial "two by four" over and over and over again.

There is only one person who never gives up...

The eternal, immortal, steadfast, patient, loving God.

Listen to these wonderful wooing words of Psalm 121...

"I lift up my eyes to the hills.
    From where does my help come?

² My help comes from the Lord,
   Who made heaven and earth.
³ He will not let your foot be moved;
   he who keeps you will not slumber.
⁴ Behold, he who keeps Israel
   will neither slumber nor sleep.
⁵ The Lord is your keeper;
   The Lord is your shade on your right hand.
⁶ The sun shall not strike you by day,
   nor the moon by night.
⁷ The Lord will keep you from all evil;
   he will keep your life.
⁸ The Lord will keep
   your going out and your coming in
   from this time forth and forevermore." (Psalm 121:1-8 ESV)

Whether you are going out or coming in...
The Lord runs to you...
He never gives up...

Seeing God At Work Every Day

The Lord will keep your going out and your coming in
from this time forth and forevermore. (Psalm 121:8 ESV)

Have you ever wondered if there was a time in your life where God gave up on you?

Have you ever given up on someone? Who? Why?

Have you ever tried to run away from God? How do you respond to the incredible fact that God runs after you and toward you in His efforts to let you know that He never gives up on you?

Is there anyone in your life that you need to "run after?"

Today marks the end of the *"Seeing God At Work Every Day– The 40 Day Challenge!"*
Congratulations!!

I would love to know in what new ways and/or in what old ways you are able to see God at work every day. Feel free to email me at David@ seeinggodatworkeveryday.com

My hope and prayer is that you will keep the eyes and ears of your heart wide open so that you may continue to experience firsthand – **"Seeing God At Work Every Day!"**

One last word of assurance for you that you can hold on to for a lifetime...

God never gives up!

About the Author

My name is David Dendy and I am truly amazed that you have taken the time to read my book:

Seeing God At Work Every Day – The 40 Day Challenge.

I have been blessed with a life that has spanned over half a century. Like a roller coaster, my life has had extreme highs, incredible dips, rapid revolutions and even a few corkscrews intertwined with gravity defying loops. What I have found to be the most intriguing part of the journey is that I follow a God who has made himself to be known through the person of Jesus Christ and in the midst of this roller coaster ride, Jesus chooses to sit next to me with his hands holding on for dear life as we both experience this white knuckle ride of a lifetime.

I have had the immense joy and privilege of being an ordained pastor for over 26 years. I have worked within in the church, outside the church and everywhere else in between. I am here to say, contrary to popular belief among many Christians and secularists alike, God has never been more at work than He is today.

I have been amazed over the years to hear from Christians and non-Christians alike that, "God is not a work anymore." I couldn't disagree more. I have found it humbling and yet delightful to see God at work every day.

This is where my book "Seeing God At Work Every Day - The 40 Day Challenge" comes into play. I spent one full year, count 'em...365 days, writing down where I saw God at work each and every day. My book takes a look at 40 of those days and then challenges us to reflect, think, pray and act upon such observations so that we too just might see God at work in our own and other's lives.

I am privileged to be married to Julie, whose passion is to help people become whole, be it mentally, spiritually, emotionally or physically. She is the best Physical Therapist I know and she is currently working with those who suffer from brain injuries. Her patience, compassion and gentle touch are unmatched.

We have two precious children, Faith (9) and Joshua (9)! They are only five months apart in age. They both love to push each other's buttons and watch the fireworks begin. And once the fireworks have fizzled they do actually love each other...

Together we do our best to exemplify, model and share the grace, mercy, forgiveness and love of Jesus with all whom we meet and encounter. Through that we have the complete joy of:

Seeing God At Work Every Day!

Laugh often and Fear not!
David!